From one surprise the "magical" story is impossible for me ... the joy inside of me as I feel an intense light has flooded my whole being, putting before me a panoramic vision of extraordinary horizons about human life, love, and the magnificent Author of the story: our magisterial and masterful God.

It brought to mind the words of Isaiah 40:9-14 that proclaims, "You who bring good news to Zion, go up on a high mountain. You who bring good news to Jerusalem, lift up your voice with a shout, lift it up, do not be afraid; say to the towns of Judah, 'Here is your God!' See, the Sovereign Lord comes with power, and he rules with a mighty arm. See, his reward is with him, and his recompense accompanies him. He tends his flock like a shepherd: He gathers the lambs in his arms and carries them close to his heart; he gently leads those that have young. Who has measured the waters in the hollow of his hand, or with the breadth of his hand marked off the heavens? Who has held the dust of the earth in a basket, or weighed the mountains on the scales and the hills in a balance? Who can fathom the Spirit of the Lord, or instruct the Lord as his counselor? Whom did the Lord consult to enlighten him, and who taught him the right way? Who was it that taught him knowledge, or showed him the path of understanding?"

I infinitely bless God for His continued presence in the love that He has for us. I bless the magical story of this four-leaf clover with a small big heart at its center. I bless each and every one of those who will read these pages and will find answers, signals, and invitations to live in a new and different way.

P. Eduardo Ramos Pons
Misioneros del Espiritu Santo, Guadalajara, Mexico

Andrés and Marysol's engaging book, *A Four-Leaf Clover: A Harbinger of Miracles*, is a brutally honest must-read testimony for singles and married couples seeking to hold fast to their Christian faith.

Whether you are reaching out to someone with severe disabilities or this describes your child, these stories will supercharge your hope! From when they first met, to later becoming a couple with young adult children, the Malos' share powerful, cross-cultural relational insights. They disclose their spiritual journey from having God in their head to a moving and personal relationship that impacts every choice they make. Speaking from great authority drawn from life's tough experiences, this couple has significant impact on marriages and families as they call others to dare and believe—far beyond what the physical eye can see.

Kathy Stoltzfus
Director, Leadership MetaFormation.com, Life Coach,
and manager of Coach22.com

Faith works through love. Love sees God's grace at work through all of life's circumstances and lives with hope-filled expectation for promise fulfilled. Andrés and Marysol demonstrate the greatness of God's love and compassion daily in their family, the Church, and to all who need an encounter with God's love and power. Their book, *A Four-Leaf Clover: A Harbinger of Miracles*, will inspire and invite you to trust God completely when situations seem hopeless and impossible. The book is a story of their love for each other, their family, and of their precious son Jesús, born with no eyes or nose. Jesús, loved and valued by God, this precious family, and many others, is a testimony of God's love and grace to a world that often devalues those with disabilities. I've watched Jesús in worship and prayer, active, engaged, and sensitive to God's presence—in this realm he has no limitations and perhaps "sees" clearer than most. *A Four-Leaf Clover: A Harbinger of Miracles* tells the amazing story of this trusting family and miracle child—read and be inspired and blessed!

Dr. Bob Sawvelle
Founding and Senior Pastor, Passion Church, Tucson, AZ
Author, *Receive Your Miracle Now: A Case for Healing Today.*

In our walk with God, my wife and I have learned that He gives special children to special parents, and we identify ourselves with this beautiful story that Andrés and Marysol share with us about their son Jesús, who has inspired us greatly. God has given us the privilege of knowing the Malo family for several years and something that really impacted our lives has been the tenderness shown in this marriage and home and the joy that they impart to the others. I am convinced that not everyone has that ability to smile transparently in the middle of the fire like the Malo family.

This book is more than a recapitulation of thoughts or concepts learned; it is a masterpiece. This book is the living and spectacular testimony of a family that has believed God. I hope you can be encouraged, comforted, restored, and grow supernaturally when reading the pages of this book. You truly have a four-leaf clover in your hands.

David Scarpeta
Senior Pastor, Grace Community Church, Houston, TX

Get ready for a heartwarming look into the special and unique lives of Andrés, Marysol, Paz, Jesús, and Sofi Malo. Their story of heartache and hope will challenge your understanding of faith. I believe you will come away with a fresh and greater awe of our Creator and Savior Jesus Christ. Jesús, their special needs son, is truly another "masterpiece" of God's making!

Dennis Watson
Gallup Certified Strengths Coach, Poiema LLC, Tucson, AZ

Life brings different challenges to each person which are answered differently. Andrés and Marysol decided to respond to their challenge with strength, love, and determination. Despite all the fears and difficulties, and the pain they felt, from the first moment they knew that their son was a unique gift from God. They were blessed to have found a four-leaf clover. One in a million. Beyond the questions, this beautiful marriage chose to give life although science, reason, and friends told them that they should chose death. For them, abortion was not an option. We have seen this family closely. We met Jesús Andrés when he was still a little boy, surrounded by the love of their parents and sisters. Against all odds, he has grown and developed many skills, but above all, he has given and received the greatest of all gifts: the love of his family. *A Four-Leaf Clover: A Harbinger of Miracles* is a wonderful story of unconditional love that will touch the depths of your heart, bringing strength and hope to your life.

Jimmy and Aída de Cornejo
Pastors of Christian Center of Cuenca, Ecuador

I have known Andrés and Marysol for over ten years and have watched them grow as a family in their relationship with God. I am so glad that they have so masterfully written the story of their incredible journey of faith. As you read this compelling story of a boy born blind, God will open your eyes to see and expect His miracles in your own life. I know your heart will be deeply touched and I highly recommend this book to you.

Craig Hill
Founder, Family Foundations International

A Four-Leaf Clover: A Harbinger of Miracles is a book that everyone needs to read. The journey of Marysol and Andrés is one of passionate pursuit, trust, and surrender. Their family's decision to continue to seek first the love of Christ in the middle of some of the most difficult medical diagnoses of their son, Jesús, is a testimony of faith that releases hope! We press on to believe for Jesús' miracle, but his life lived out daily is already a miracle and testimony to the glory of our great God and King, Jesus Christ.

Pastor Joanne Miles Moody
Agape Freedom Fighters

A Four-Leaf Clover

A Harbinger of Miracles

Frank & Olivia,
Dare to see beyond.
Feb 11:1
Andrés Malo

ANDRÉS & MARYSOL MALO

Adam Colwell's writeworks

Edited by Adam Colwell, Adam Colwell's WriteWorks, LLC
Cover design by Rich Steele, Harvest Media Ministries
Interior design and typesetting by Katherine Lloyd, THE DESK

Printing and distribution through Family Foundations International

Print ISBN: 978-1-7324474-0-0
eBook ISBN: 978-1-7324474-1-7

To our two incredible daughters: Paz and Sofi.
Each of you are a gift from God for us. You both arrived
in the perfect timing to convey the love of God in an
unprecedented way. We are so proud of you and we
appreciate your tender hearts to be part of the special
family we are. We love you!

To our Lord Jesus Christ,
In Whom we are found and without Him
we can do nothing. We love you, Jesus!

Acknowledgments

We want to give special thanks to our families in Ecuador and in Mexico:

To our Papón Heron, who went to meet our Father in Heaven while we were writing this book.

To our Moms, Norita and Aidita.

To our Brothers and Sisters: Jorge, Silvia, Raúl, Eduardo, Yiye, Guimi, Isabel, Patty, Arturo, Maria Caridad, Pepe, and Pilo.

To our nephews and nieces: Raúl Andrés, Jorge, Dani, José Adrian, Elisa, Juan José, Carla, Mario, Martín, Evita, Martina, Emi, and Sere.

A special thanks to Grandfather Guillermo and Chiqui, who since our son Jesús was born gave us his support to help us offer him a better future. Also, to our Mama Alicia, or Shisha, the first one who believed in Jesús' miracle.

Also, to Linda Patten, and all the teachers, aides, caregivers, and nurses that have poured out love and care into Jesús' life and our family.

Also, to Jim and Linda Floyd and *Familia Bonilla Cevallos*, two of many other families who have intimately embraced us as their own family.

Also, we want to acknowledge and give a great thanks to the family of the faith that we have had the privilege to know and be part of. You all have opened your hearts to us: *Misioneros del Espíritu Santo*, Family Foundations International, *Centro Cristiano de Cuenca, Unsion TV, Centro Cristiano Carismático,* Beth Sar Shalom, Grace Church, Celebration Church, Oasis Church, *Casa de Adoración,* Passion Church, and Harvest Media Ministries.

When I was very young, my mother told me that if you find a four-leaf clover, you are going to have great luck. Anything can happen; it's magical.

In Cuenca, Ecuador, where I grew up, there is grass everywhere. I used to spend hours playing near my house, always looking for that elusive clover of good fortune. I'd think that maybe today, I'll find it. It was an obsession.

Experts claim there is one four-leaf clover for every ten thousand three-leaf shamrocks. One in ten thousand!

I never found a four-leaf clover.

Years later, when my wife Marysol gave birth to our son, Jesús Andrés Malo, he had two uncommon disorders at the same time. In the first months of his life, he was in critical condition. We talked to many doctors as he was treated at the top hospital for child disorders in Latin America. Every one of those doctors told us, time and again, that Jesús was an unusual child; one in a million. That's far rarer than even a four-leaf clover.

Allow Marysol and me to introduce you to our son—our four-leaf clover.

We pray his story will prove magical for you.

Chapter 1

"I'm missing the eyes..."

Marysol

When you're pregnant, you always want to think everything is going to be fine. You never want to think something is going to go wrong or be life-threatening.

Four months earlier, my mother was with me when we learned my unborn child was a boy, and we heard his heartbeat for the first time. At that time, my husband Andrés was away from home for a family need, but when I called him with the news, he was so happy. We were both thrilled because a son was going to be a perfect match for Paz, our daughter who was born the previous summer.

Andrés provided a wonderful life for us in Cuenca. He was a hard worker as a salesperson in his grandfather Guillermo's jewelry store—a faithful man with a heart filled with love for me and our daughter. Now I was going to give him a son—*Lentejito*, we called him at first, because the doctor said he was the size of a lentil. I was overjoyed by the life growing within me.

Then came the day when as a couple we returned to the doctor. I was in my seventh month of pregnancy, and I was excited

Andrés was going to have a chance to hear our son's heartbeat for himself.

The day is forever chiseled into my memory. October 4, 2000.

Andrés

Marysol was the woman of my dreams. That we became husband and wife after everything we went through—everything she endured from me—and started a family with Paz was, in itself, amazing. When she told me we were going to have a son, I didn't know I had more room inside of me for so much love, so much fullness and joy. Somehow, I did, and I was overflowing as we journeyed to the doctor so that I could hear the beating heart of my precious *Lentejito*.

We entered the exam room. It was small and sterile, darkened so that the sonogram would be clearly visible. Marysol was told to change into a hospital gown and then lie down on the bed, where she was briskly prepped for the procedure. I stood next to my bride. She looked so beautiful, so expectant—and then there it was. *Whoosh-whoosh. Whoosh-whoosh.* The heartbeat of our son. Firm and steady.

I looked to the doctor, expecting to see a smile, but his expression was at first hard to read, and then suddenly clear as could be. Confusion. Like he couldn't believe what he was seeing. Or not seeing.

"I'm missing the eyes—I'm missing the eyes," he said. "I don't see the nose, either."

Marysol

I was expecting good news, and my anticipation grew when I heard the heartbeat pounding so strongly and saw the smile on

Andrés's face. He has such a handsome smile; it beams forth his boyish charm and reminds me of the first day I saw it and was captured by it. Then I heard the doctor's words. Jarring and cold. No mother wants to hear words like those. I covered my eyes. The sobs came.

Moments later, the doctor said he was going to his office, and told us to wait. Wait? How could we possibly wait when we were just told the baby had—what? No eyes? No nose? What does that even mean? Andrés began cleaning the gel from my stomach. He then reached over and helped me up so I could get dressed. I appreciated his touch just then. For the moment, his touch seemed to be all I had. That, and the unmistakable life within me.

What was going to happen to him? To us?

Andrés

I took Marysol in my arms and together we walked from the exam room to the doctor's office. She was trembling. I'm sure I was, too, but what little focus I had at that moment was on her. *Surely*, I thought, *he'll have answers, a plan or procedures to follow that will allow us to help our son, perhaps even reverse the problems.* We were instructed to go inside.

> Only God can determine life.

He was silent as we sat down. Then he spoke. He didn't give us answers. Instead, he rendered a judgment.

"In these cases," he said, "the Church allows—"

He wasn't given the chance to complete his sentence, or to say the next word that we not only did not wish to hear but refused to accept. *Life belongs to God*, I spoke to my heart, and was about to speak, but I didn't need to say a word. Marysol's eyes expressed our shared disagreement with him.

Marysol

Abortion was not an option. Only God can determine life. We were looking for hope from the doctor and received anything but. We stood up, and with a quick goodbye, left his office.

If God wanted our son to be born, he would be, no matter what. Our boy was alive! We believed he came from God as a blessing to us. Two weeks later, we gave him a name. Jesús. It came when we were on our living room couch, leaning into each other, holding one another. It was one of those despairing moments that came easily in those early days after the diagnosis. We didn't know what to do, what to think, or even how to pray. That night, all we did was hug and cry out to God.

"Jesus—Jesus—Jesus," we pleaded.

Then it happened. I spoke, "We will name him Jesús." Andrés looked at me. "Yes, yes," he said. There was an instant sense of peace—the first peace we'd felt since learning of his condition. In time, we'd realize that by naming our son Jesús, we actually set him aside and gave him to God.

But that was later. In the moment we left the doctor's office and drove home, I knew nothing of peace—and we were about to discover things were only going to get worse.

Andrés

When the doctor so coldly told us our son's condition, Marysol and I knew enough about God to know we could cry out to him, but not much more. She was born and raised as a Catholic, so she always had that godly tradition in her life. As for me, it wasn't until I was nineteen that I had an encounter with God and knew that He existed, and even then, my faith was fleeting. I never found a good church, never read my Bible. In my twenties, I did meditation and yoga as part of a random sort of search for spirituality, but it wasn't until Marysol and I were married that I began rediscovering God in my life.

That's not surprising when you consider that it was with Marysol, during our first summer when we fell in love, that I spoke of God as anything more than an idea.

The warmth of that lovely summer was a long distant memory as I went to work the following day. I had to go; it was late in the year, a time when sales were vital, but I was nothing more than a zombie. I hardly knew how to get from one place to another. There was a fog in my heart. It was so hard to see little Pazita talking so clearly and brilliantly, knowing she was going to be a big sister of a special boy who would be only able to—what? Would he even be able to talk properly? I had no idea what a child with my son's disorders could do or could not do. At work, I noticed for the first time how everyone had a nose. It was ridiculously absurd and profoundly sad. And, of course, it was unbearable to see Marysol suffer. I wanted to help her feel better, see her smile, give her hope. But I had nothing to give because I had so little information to work with.

I knew we had to get a second opinion and, hopefully, better insight about our son. My siblings lived in the capital city of Quito, and my oldest sister Silvia referred us to one of the best pediatricians in the country. We made plans for the trip, but it would have to wait until after I returned from an already-scheduled sales trip to Guayaquil. I couldn't cancel, but it was the last thing I wanted to do.

Marysol

All of my family was in Mexico, so when Andrés was at work I was home with Paz—and no one else. Andrés was always there for me, always enough, but now? The uncertainty was so pervasive and the heartbreak so acute, half of my heart was gone. When Andrés had to leave for the sales trip, I couldn't help but feel abandoned, I was so lonely. Paz was there, of course, and she lifted my spirit because she was so full of life and happy; she brought me relief. But she was too little to understand, and certainly too small to share the suffering, even though I could sense she knew something was wrong. It was too much to bear by myself.

I couldn't wait for Andrés to return home so that we wouldn't be alone. I couldn't wait for him to return, too, because I couldn't wait to leave. Perhaps in Quito we would get some answers.

Andrés

During the flight to Guayaquil, it was as though the plane cabin was closing in on me, my despair was so deep. I knew I needed to talk to someone, anyone, about what was happening in my life.

"Do you believe in God?" I asked the man sitting next to me.

"Yes, profoundly," he responded. I then let it all pour out—about the exam room, the doctor's words, our reaction, and our fears. I already knew that he was a doctor, and he went on to detail how deformities in unborn children could be caused by many things, such as tomatoes. *Great*, I thought. *He means well, I'm sure, but here's another doctor telling me something that isn't helping.*

The sales trip couldn't end fast enough. It was a blur, nothing more, and as soon as I returned home, we left our daughter Paz with our neighbor Tia Marujita, and Marysol and I boarded an early morning flight to Quito. When we arrived, we went to Silvia's home so that we could use her car to go to the clinic. We were desperate. We wanted to hear something different. We wanted to hear that *Lentejito's* condition was not as bad as we were told.

Our first stop that morning was to a gynecologist. She did another sonogram and saw the same things the first doctor had seen, but her only comment was that the baby had a strong heart—a fact that entered immediately into my heart, telling me my son was going to live. From there, we went to the pediatric clinic. It was in a residential area in a house that was converted into medical offices and had a nice view of the city. While the doctor recommended by my sister was not there, we were introduced to another person who we were assured was a specialist in the type of cases we were facing. He was a tall man, professional, with a larger-than-normal office. He welcomed us, and I was encouraged.

> We were desperate. We wanted to hear something different.

Now we'll find out something useful. We showed him the sonogram from the gynecologist. "What do you think?" I asked.

He hesitated. "These babies come with challenges. I know the problems these babies bring to families. These problems are complicated." He seemed to be struggling to find the right words. The doctor touched his own nose and eyes. "These parts aren't there."

Then he said, "He's like a monster."

Marysol

My ears functioned, because I heard the words. They formed meaning in my brain. I understood them. But I wouldn't allow myself to accept them.

"He's a little monster," the doctor said again, adding that even if he lived through birth, he'd have to be put on machines to survive.

"If it were my baby," he concluded, "I would have an abortion."

They told us this man had a background in special needs cases. They led us to believe he was the best of the best.

They were wrong.

Andrés leaned close to me. "We don't need to listen to this man for one more second. *He's* the monster!" I'd never heard him so indignant. I agreed with him.

We grabbed the VHS tape of the sonogram and left. We drove back to Silvia's house, dropped off the car, and returned directly to the airport. That afternoon, we got on the plane and slumped into our seats. I looked at Andrés and saw utter exhaustion. I couldn't imagine how I looked, but I was so empty inside it's entirely possible I was invisible.

> "What is life going to be like for him?" I couldn't fathom it.

Why didn't they have answers?

We were in Cuenca by evening. Our Paz was well cared for by Tía Marujita. It was a joy to see Paz full of life and energy. Nevertheless, my inner emptiness hindered me from enjoying her as much as I wanted.

Andrés

Back home, we didn't know what to do next. I told my family what happened in Quito and what else we learned, if you want to call it that. Some asked if we were considering abortion. I wasn't offended, but I firmly told them "No." They offered to help in any way we needed. I appreciated that, but I had no idea how they could help. I really had no idea about anything.

My grandfather's birthday was coming, so I went to the store to get him a card. I scanned the racks, looking for something appropriate—and my vision blurred. Tears. I started to cry. I realized my son would never be able to read a card. The doctor's words echoed in my mind: *I'm missing the eyes.* I almost walked out. I didn't want to buy a card. I didn't want anything except for my son to be okay.

Marysol

Desolation. That was all I knew. I felt hopelessness. My mother's reaction to the news was sadness, but she didn't know what to say, and no one from my family in Mexico could come to see me. I stayed inside my home, doted over Paz, and was aware every moment of the baby living, growing inside of me. He was precious, so very precious, but fear was my constant companion. All I could think was, "What is life going to be like for him?" I couldn't fathom it.

Then I heard the news from Andrés. Specialists were coming to Cuenca as part of a program called Smile Surgery. These doctors performed free surgeries on people with cleft palate or cleft lip. Two were from Canada, and the other was from the United States.

Surely, we could see them; surely, they could tell us what to do for our son. We needed to know. His due date was just weeks away.

Chapter 2

"Me for You, You for Me, and for Forever."

Marysol

It's funny what happens when you look back in time. You realize that, back then, there was no way you could have predicted the joys and trials to come—especially if you're in love's first bloom.

My hometown of Querétaro in central Mexico is considered today to offer the best quality of life and to be one of the safest cities in the nation. It was certainly no different back when I was a nineteen-year-old university student. Querétaro is an old colonial town turned urban center that retained the geometric street plan of the Spanish conquerors side-by-side with the twisting alleys of the native Otomi people. Fern-filled jacaranda trees are everywhere. The sunsets are stunning. It's the ideal place to fall in love.

Not that I was all that interested in love. I'd only had one boyfriend up to that point and it was a terrible experience. I was focused instead on my marketing studies at the *Tecnológico de Monterrey* in Mexico City, and in the summer of 1989, I was spending a few months in Querétaro with my family. One hot Saturday, my ten-year-old cousin Alejandra wanted to go swimming, so we went to the pool at the university. We arrived and saw we had the pool all to ourselves.

Except for one person.

Andrés

I was in Querétaro taking classes at the *Tecnológico de Monterrey* after arriving from Guaymas. My pursuit of a degree in biochemical engineering allowed me to take classes in cities throughout Mexico, and this was my next stop before heading back to Guaymas. I liked to take a swim each Saturday at the university pool.

I was already doing my laps in the water when I noticed two other people at the end of the pool. They must have arrived when I wasn't looking. One was a little girl wearing a cute pink one-piece. The other person was in a one-piece as well, midnight blue, and she had swim goggles around her neck, her brown hair draped loose over her shoulders.

> I was captured.
> A beautiful white swan,
> I thought to myself.

I was captured. *A beautiful white swan*, I thought to myself.

I wasn't one to up and approach a girl, but I knew I had to be bold. I swam toward her to the other corner of the pool. The child was doing flips and didn't acknowledge my arrival. I stopped and stood on the bottom, still chest deep in the water, and faced the woman. She was even lovelier up close.

"Hello," I said. She responded accordingly. "Do you study here?"

"No," she said. "I'm studying at the campus in Mexico City. But I am here spending the summer with my family." I thought I could get lost in her gorgeous eyes. I followed their gaze as she looked to her right. "This is my cousin, Alejandra." The child smiled at me, then took another plunge.

Keep talking, I thought. "What are you studying?"

"Marketing," she said. "And you?"

"Biochemistry. For food processing." As I paused, I noticed my heart was pounding, and not from my laps. "What is your name?

"I'm Marysol."

"I'm Andrés. Nice to meet you." I stretched out my arm to shake her hand.

Marysol

I wanted to laugh. I saw he wanted to shake my hand, but his forearm was still underneath the water. It was funny. It was also sweet, and I liked his accent. I shook his hand. "Nice to meet you."

We made more small talk, but more influential than his conversation was the peaceful sensation I experienced from him. Perhaps it was his Ecuadorian manners. Maybe it was his smile. But it made me feel special.

"What would you do if I invited you to a movie?" he asked.

I didn't see the oddly-worded date request coming, but I didn't mind it, either. "I'd say 'Yes.'"

"May I have your phone number to call you?"

The numbers just flowed, unhesitant. "I will call you. Goodbye." He swam across the pool and did a couple more laps. I tried to turn my attention back to Alejandra. A few minutes later, I saw Andrés come out of the changing room wearing shorts and a white t-shirt. He was fit, slim, and the sun shone off his brown hair like gold.

"Chao!" he said as he walked by.

Chao, not Adios, I thought. *Hmmm. And he's pretty cute, too.*

A Four-Leaf Clover

Andrés

For the rest of my swim, I kept repeating to myself, *Ocho-cero-cero-cuarenta. Ocho-cero-cero-cuarenta.* I wasn't going to forget that number. Two days later, I called her. Our first date was set. I decided to take her to see the movie The Big Blue at the theater in the Plaza del Parque, and then to dinner in the city center. Downtown Querétaro was a great place to be with someone, a place to walk and get to know them. That's what I wanted to do with Marysol. I desired to learn everything I could about this woman.

The drive to Marysol's house in the rustic Jurica neighborhood took fifteen minutes, but I kept wishing time would speed up. I couldn't wait to get there. My journey ended on a street made of little stones. Trees were all around, and the house had a large, lush yard. My senses were heightened, almost like I was seeing all these sights for the first time. I was impressed by Marysol, and amazed she said, "Yes." I tried to ignore the lightness in my chest as I got out of the car and walked toward the door.

Marysol

I was at the window, sitting and looking out with my grandma, when his car pulled into the driveway. I got an empty feeling in the pit of my stomach. *I'm going out with this person, and I don't even know him.* Part of me wanted to flee out the back door like a frightened schoolgirl. When my mother greeted him at the door, she came into the side room where I was keeping out of sight.

"He's fine, Marysol. Go. Have fun."

With her words, that same sense of calm I felt at the pool two days earlier returned. I went out to meet him, and we walked side-by-side to the car. He held the passenger door open for me as I got in. Like a gentleman.

The movie was great. The dinner afterward was exceptional,

and not just because of the cuisine or the romantic outdoor table he chose for us. I was completely happy with this charming man. Even more, I appreciated his tenderness. Andrés was a type of man I'd never experienced before.

Andrés

We walked downtown, where there are many narrow passages and amazing architecture. Marysol wouldn't allow me to hold her hand as we strolled, and I thought her choice was beautiful because she was so reserved. In the days to come, my friends at the university started saying that my relationship with Marysol was my "white friendship" because it was so pure. In the following weeks, we continued our walks in the city or in her neighborhood. It was then that we cemented our caring for one another. We also discussed something that I never before shared with anyone: God and His importance in my life.

I wasn't falling in love, like it was a process. I *was* in love. Instantaneously. I understood that Marysol was a woman like no other.

Marysol

We had our playful moments, too, during those delightful two months—at least, I know it was playful for me. Practically every morning, we played tennis at the university. The night before, we always agreed to meet at my home at 8:30 a.m. Then I'd sit and stew: 8:45 a.m., then nine o'clock, then a quarter after. Finally, usually around 9:45 a.m., Andrés would show up, smiling and uttering his apologies for being late, and we'd then head to the university to play.

His tardiness was like clockwork, but so was my annoyance. I was so mad that I took it out on him on the court. I was a better player than he—an advantage that allowed me to toy with him as I pleased. I intentionally hit volleys to the left corner baseline, then over to the right and back again. I'd throw in a lob here and there after chasing him forward to the net with a little chip shot. I ran him all over the place.

Did Andrés get angry at losing all the time? Sure—but I didn't care. I wanted to punish him. I'd let him get in a few shots and sometimes allow him to be on the verge of a game point, and then I'd pull it away. I always beat him in the end. He only won a game once, and he knew it was because I let him.

It was so fun. We both loved the teasing.

Andrés

Of course, I had my ways of getting back at Marysol for her beat down on the tennis court. One of our favorite restaurants was the Archangel, so named because of a picture inside the dining room of an angel with a dark orange face and metallic wings, a piece of art characteristic of what was produced in that area. Marysol loved drinking carrot juice, so much so that it was not unusual for her hands to have an orange tint to them from holding the glass so often. At the Archangel, I'd call her my "bunny" and chide her that she needed to get more juice so that she could become as orange as the angel.

I know—it wasn't much, but I had to lampoon her in some way to soothe my tennis ego. Really, I teased her just to see that flicker of fire in her eyes, because it was always followed by a twinkle and a smile that never ceased to melt my heart.

Marysol

The thing about Andrés is that he courted me—always inviting me to places, constantly providing for me, unending in his generosity. It was overwhelming, and I loved every moment. What made him most attractive to me, though, was that he knew God existed. We spent hours talking about God, inviting Him into our conversation naturally, without even thinking about it. I could tell Andrés had a reverence for God like I did. I just knew God was vital to me. I wanted to please God with my life, and Andrés shared that passion.

> I wanted to please God with my life, and Andrés shared that passion.

Andrés had something special, a freedom that I saw in him that I couldn't see in other guys. It was very attractive, and that more than anything caused me to fall in love with Andrés—and would make what was about to happen next that much more heartbreaking.

I knew Andrés was leaving. He had to return to Guaymas for school at the same time my classes were starting again in Mexico City. Three days before our summer together ended, we were at a restaurant and I wrote on the napkin, "Are we boyfriend and girlfriend?" You'd think I'd have known intuitively, but we hadn't even held hands yet, much less kissed one another. I was also protecting myself, still hurting from my earlier boyfriend experience. Since then, I'd kept boys at a distance. Until Andrés.

Andrés read the napkin and smiled, not in a teasing way, but somehow understanding that I was seriously seeking an answer to my question. He assured me he was my boyfriend. That set me at ease. Later, we attended a friend's wedding together, and after the ceremony we went dancing. As good as I was at tennis, Andrés was that much better as a dancer. He knew all the steps, executed all the moves with precision. He was excellent, and as his partner he made me feel like I was dancing wonderfully. Many of the dances involved holding hands, and I was now more than happy to let him.

When that evening came to a close, he took me aside to a private nook near that club, embraced my hands in his, and we kissed for the very first time. It was long and sweet. I was so in the clouds.

We went our separate ways, and in the first weeks of school my classmates in Mexico City couldn't stop asking what had happened to me that summer, the change was so evident. I wrote letters to Andrés filled with details of my days and how much I missed him. I couldn't wait to hear back from him.

A month passed, and then a second. October arrived, and I still hadn't heard from Andrés. He never wrote, never called. *What did I do?* I ruminated. *Was I just a fling to him? He never treated me that way then. Why isn't he courting me now?* My heart plunged. There were nights when I'd sit and look at all the photos we took of each other during that summer and waver back and forth between sadness and disillusionment.

Finally, I received a call. It was Andrés. "How are you?" he says, his tone bright as a chime, like nothing was wrong. I didn't know what to say, so I asked the obvious.

"Have you missed me?"

"No."

He went on to talk about how his classes were going, how difficult the schoolwork was, and how he sometimes went diving at the nearby beach. I never asked him why he hadn't responded to my letters. At that point, it hardly mattered.

"I'm going to return to Querétaro," he said. "Next semester."

"Do whatever you want," I responded, purposefully deadpan. I hoped he felt the chill over the phone line. "I don't care."

I hung up. The clang of the receiver on the phone matched the sound of my heart's door closing.

Andrés

When she hung up, I felt the coldness—and confusion. *Okay, so I said, "no,"* I reasoned. *But that isn't because I don't miss her.* In reality, I missed Marysol so desperately it was affecting everything I was doing. Back when I started university studies in Mexico, I was homesick for Ecuador. My mother and father were getting a divorce, and as the second youngest of five children, I was concerned about leaving my siblings in that mess. I was so wounded by what was happening with my family I talked with a priest to try to figure things out. At the same time, both my father and grandfather were paying for my university expenses. It was no small sum. Therefore, when I started school, I did everything I could to set Ecuador aside, compartmentalizing it away from my mind and heart so I could focus. It was the only way I could concentrate on succeeding at school. Try as I might, I failed organic chemistry. Retaking that course was how I ended up in Querétaro for the summer, met Marysol, and fell in love.

Marysol was all I could think about when I returned to Guaymas and, again, my attention to school waned. I decided the only way I could pass my classes was to take Marysol, just like I had Ecuador, and set her aside. I couldn't even think about her. If I did, there was nothing else. I didn't answer her letters. I avoided calling to not be distracted by the sweet sound of her voice. Finally, when I couldn't stand it any longer, I did call. And it was true—I hadn't missed her. If I'd allowed myself the indulgence of missing her, even for a moment, it would've utterly consumed me.

I did return to Querétaro the next semester, and I tried to court Marysol again on the weekends she visited her parents. But it was different. She was so much more mature and responsible than I was. She kept me at a distance, and I lingered there on the fringes like a lost puppy hoping for a bone. I was still so in love with her. The time for her graduation in Mexico City arrived, but I was so homesick for my family in Ecuador that I chose to go and visit them over seeing her graduate. When I returned from Ecuador, even the fringes seemed off limits. When we were together, she treated me like a mom. "Put on your coat, Andrés," she'd say. I wanted her to be like my friends' girlfriends, going to parties and having fun. We argued often. I longed to be with her but started dreading every visit. So, I made what seemed to me a reasonable proposition.

"Let's take a break," I told her one night on the way home in the car. It was an innocent idea; we could take a month or two, not see each other, and then come back together and see if we got along any better.

She started to cry.

Marysol

I felt like he was breaking up with me—and why wouldn't he? He wouldn't communicate with me like a normal boyfriend. He came back to Querétaro, but I never seemed to be what he wanted me to be. I wasn't a party girl. I didn't want to be like his friends' girlfriends. He didn't even go to my graduation. I'd call him a child, and even treat him like one because that's how he acted.

"This is going nowhere," I told him. Later, when we met and he begged me to take him back, I said he was a *veleta*, a sailboat without a captain that goes wherever the wind takes him. One of my brothers asked me why I was even meeting with Andrés; after all, he was just going to eventually return to Ecuador. I thought they had a point.

"Someday," I told him. "Maybe in a couple of years we can talk."

I saw his pained stare. It was clear he was still in love with me. The problem was that we didn't know *how* to be in love with each other. At the end, he said, "I hope someday I will get married to someone like you."

We separated. I went to work in marketing at Kellogg's in Querétaro. He finished school, worked for a while in Mexico, and then headed back to Ecuador. Over the next few

> I never forgot our summer and the tenderness he showed.

years, the only time we talked was when he would call my home every Valentine's Day. The calls were bittersweet; we'd make small talk, but nothing more. I could sense he wanted to say something more, but he could never get the words out.

I'd hardened my heart to Andrés, but I never forgot our summer and the tenderness he showed.

Andrés

Without Marysol, my life went into a horrible spiral. I was miserable. Every Valentine's Day call I wanted to say it: *I love you.* But the words would lodge in my throat. I dated other girls and was even with one woman for a year and a half. In the end, though, I had to break up with that woman. "I don't want to hurt you," I said to her. "I'm still in love with a girl back in Mexico." I couldn't fall in love with anyone else, no matter how hard I tried.

I only loved Marysol.

In all, five years passed. Then came another call in January 1996. It changed everything.

Marysol

When I picked up the phone and heard his voice, I was confused. After all, it wasn't Valentine's Day. But as caught off guard as I was at the call itself, his words were even more unexpected.

He asked about me and my family, but then he revealed, "I don't know what is going on with me. I cannot fall in love, and I'm hurting others."

There it was again; the tenderness. "But what can I do?" I responded softly. "I am here, and you are there." We talked some more and agreed to stay in touch. His call was significant because, unknown to Andrés, I was in a pivotal time of my life. My job at Kellogg's had ended, as had my relationships there and with other friends away from work. The night before, I'd also received a call from my first boyfriend, the one who had treated me so poorly all of those years ago. He told me he was dying of cancer, and he asked me to forgive him for any pain he had caused me when we were together. When Andrés called, something came alive again inside of me. I'd always felt Andrés was the only person who ever truly understood me. Now here he was, calling and sharing his heart as he'd never done before.

We'd both grown. We'd changed. Now Andrés was back in touch. It was something special.

That conversation ended and a few more months passed before we talked again. This time, Andrés had a more specific reason for his call.

He was coming to see me.

Andrés

I had a very symbolic dream. It was a little traumatic, but I believe it was given to me by God. In it, I was at a table, and in the middle of the table was a gold vase with branches woven throughout it. I understood that the vase somehow represented my life, and the vase itself was transparent. I could see right through it. Then I understood that it was like my heart: it was not empty, because it contained the branches, but there was something missing. A gold piece.

When I woke up, it didn't take me long to realize what—or who—was missing. That morning, I purchased two round-trip airline tickets. One was for me to get to Mexico and back. The other was for Marysol to come from there to Ecuador and back home. I called Marysol and told her I was coming to see her, but I didn't tell her about the other ticket.

Shortly after I arrived in Querétaro, a huge storm hit the city. Pedro, a former peer in college, and his wife Mari Carmen, both Ecuadorians, hosted me in their home and let me borrow their car. I drove to Marysol's home through streets so badly flooded that by the time I arrived, my ankles were wet from water coming into the car. Somehow, the vehicle didn't stall. When I sloshed up to the door and it opened, I couldn't breathe. There she was, my beautiful white swan, lovelier than ever.

The next day, her brother Pepe and her mother Aidita joined us and we went to San Miguel, a small romantic town an hour outside of Querétaro. It was wonderful, and one of our visits was to a gothic cathedral. I walked into a small nave and was joined by Marysol's mom. "So what are you doing here, Andrés?" she asked. I told her I was here to find out what was going to happen with Marysol. That seemed to be satisfactory to her. I felt like Aidita and Pepe were giving me a green light.

The day after that, we went alone into Querétaro to the Café Tulip in front of the emblematic aqueduct, a symbol of the city. We found a table and took our seats. After ordering, Marysol looked at me very firmly, leaned forward, and planted both arms flat on the table.

Entonces qué, Malo? she said. "So what, Malo?"

I didn't mind her flippant tone. It was the least I deserved.

I took out the airline ticket. "I came here to tie up everything that needs to be tied, and to loose anything that needs to be loosed." I said. "I haven't been able to forget you or fall in love with anyone else." I slid the ticket across the table to her. Her eyes widened as she read her name on the ticket. "I want you to come to Ecuador. As a friend."

> There she was, my beautiful white swan, lovelier than ever.

Marysol

At that moment, I regretted being so callous with him. It was a special gesture, but I was also scared at what it could mean. I was lonely and felt misunderstood, but Andrés was again conquering my heart.

I couldn't resist.

Andrés returned to Ecuador, and over the next four months I was again struggling. One part of me wanted to give myself fully to his love once again, but another part didn't want to get hurt. I sometimes thought it would be crazy to go all the way to Ecuador where I didn't know anyone and didn't know what was going to happen.

When it was all said and done, I got on the plane. I arrived the day after Christmas. I stayed for twelve days.

Andrés

I thought my idea was brilliant. I'd have Marysol meet my entire family, see the city of Cuenca, and get a sense of what life would be like in Ecuador. It was easy; I lived with my grandfather, so the whole clan would be there. We even set her up with her own room in the corner of the house.

Entonces qué, Malo? I'd show her.

But, like so many of my past ideas about Marysol, I seemed to be missing the point. We were hardly alone, and after a while I figured out that she wanted to be with *me*—not everyone else. Besides, I wanted to ask her to marry me and find the perfect way to do it. Near the end of the dozen days, I overheard one of my uncles ask her what was happening with the two of us. "I don't know," she said. "I'm just going to leave and go back home."

I have no idea if she knew I was within earshot, but I got the message. That afternoon, we were alone at the swimming pool in the back yard. She was sitting at the side of the pool, and I was in the water.

"Marysol, I would be the happiest man on Earth if I could marry you."

Question asked, I immediately dove under the water and swam to the bottom, my plunge compelled by sudden and unforeseen embarrassment. After a while, when I had no more oxygen to spare, I surfaced.

I waited for her to speak.

Marysol

Wow, I thought. *What a dream proposal. Boy asks girl, boy dives to the bottom of a swimming pool, boy comes up panting for air, girl—*

Does what? What does a girl do to respond to an odd proposal like that?

"You need to go talk to my parents," I told him.

Of course, I wanted to say "yes," and surely should've. But, again, the strange approach Andrés chose threw me off—but not for long. Andrés dried and changed, and together we went to his grandfather's office. I knew Andrés intended to tell his grandfather that he needed to go to Mexico to ask for my parent's permission to marry me. But I beat him to the punch.

"Guillermo," I said. "We want to get married."

Andrés looked as though he was a little boy on Christmas morning. I felt much the same way.

I returned home, and then several weeks later Andrés, his grandfather Guillermo, his mother Norita, and sister Caridad traveled to Querétaro. Knowing Andrés, I told him straight out, "Surely, you are bringing me an engagement ring. I don't want you to give it to me in front of everybody."

He didn't let me down.

Andrés

I never felt such euphoria. I never dreamed before with so much intensity about my future with Marysol, so radiant, at the center of my life. I thought for hours about how I was going to give her the ring, which was handcrafted by the jewelry artisans at my grandfather's jewelry store and created from a design I had chosen. I wanted Marysol's ring to be a true work of art.

According to custom, my grandfather Guillermo was to join me when I asked Marysol's hand in marriage. He'd replace my father who had passed away three years earlier. My mom, my sister, and my grandma were also to come with me. Therefore, I imagined myself giving her the ring in front of the two families, after the formal words that are supposed to be said during the dinner. But when we arrived in Mexico City and Marysol took me aside and asked me to not give her the ring in front of everybody, that undid my original plans. But it did not lessen my enthusiasm—or my creativity.

A dinner was planned in downtown Querétaro so Marysol's family could meet with my family members near the hotel where we were staying. We chose a restaurant inside this vast, century-old colonial plaza that was two stories high, surrounded and supported by pillars. Inside the plaza was a courtyard area with many lovely little plants in pots. A couple of hours before dinner began, I went into the courtyard and saw some children singing and playing instruments. I talked to the youngsters and then picked a plant—and tucked the ring nicely under the foliage.

An hour later after the dinner and before dessert, I asked Marysol to take a walk with me. I took her into the courtyard and, right on cue, the children appeared and began performing and singing a traditional love song to Marysol. I then asked her to feel around the plant, and she found the ring. It was in a red box. She opened it, and I asked Marysol to be my wife once again.

This time, she said "yes" without hesitation. We embraced and kissed, and at that moment I knew the missing gold piece of the vase of my life was now in place.

I was complete.

Marysol

From that wonderful night, it would be another nine months before we were married in Querétaro on January 3, 1998—the promise of our summer from nine years earlier fulfilled. During the time between our engagement and the wedding, I asked Andrés to have a retreat organized for the two of us by my spiritual father Eduardo Ramos in a retreat house in San Luis Potosí. There, father Eduardo met with us for two days and nights of pre-marital counseling, and it was the first time I ever saw Andrés cry—tears of joy because he was so happy. We talked about deep issues from our past, as well as practical subjects to prepare us for married life. Our lessons came from a book, and from it we saw a phrase that we made a motto for our life together.

"Me for You, You for Me, and for Forever."

In those nine months, I planned every single detail of our religious wedding with father Eduardo. By that time, I was wholeheartedly a part of Santa Barbara community where the *Misioneros del Espiritu Santo*, the denomination that my brother Pepe belonged to, were participating to build the community in the faith, and I was so thankful to be part of it. Our wedding was celebrated in the parish of that community where twelve priests from the *Misioneros del Espiritu Santo* celebrated the wedding mass for us. They were part of my family; all of them were my brothers, and Pepe was in Spain then and could not come to the wedding. It was such a special and beautiful ceremony marked with the invitation of God into our marriage.

I completed my master's degree while Andrés returned to Ecuador and continued working while renting an apartment, which he furnished and readied for us to move into after we were married. We ended up honeymooning in Europe. I took care of everything, and we made the trip in conjunction with seeing my brother Pepe in Spain as he was ordained to be a deacon. We went to Paris and then other places in Spain. It was a dream.

Next, we moved my things from Querétaro and settled in Cuenca, where we lived for the next ten years. Andrés worked in his grandfather's watch shop while I taught college and worked in marketing for a non-profit organization benefitting women. I became pregnant with Paz nine months after we were married. When she was born, she was such a gift for me, a part of me that was uniquely mine, and I left my career to become a full-time mother. Shortly after that, I became pregnant with *Lentejito*.

It's true. Looking back, there's no way I could've predicted what would happen or how it would play out. Now, the same thing was about to come true—starting with what we were about to learn about our son from the specialists with *Operación Sonrisa* Smile Surgery.

Chapter 3

"His heart is strong."

Andrés

The specialists were staying at the Hotel El Dorado, adjacent to my grandfather Guillermo's jewelry store. We were able to see them in the evening—about 8:00 p.m., after the trio completed a long day of surgeries. They graciously gave us some of their time. We sat down in the hotel lobby, the five of us in a small circle with Marysol sitting as comfortably as she could, her beautiful pregnant belly protruding as she took her seat. Then, I played the recording of our sonogram on one of the room's large televisions.

"His heart is strong."

It was the first comment made by any of these doctors when viewing the video. *This baby is coming,* I thought. *He's going to make it.* It started to offset my greatest fear: that our son would not live.

One specialist then told us about hypoplasia, the underdevelopment or incomplete development of a tissue or an organ. She believed our son had hypoplasia of the eyes, a condition called microphthalmia, in which one or both eyeballs are abnormally small or appear to be completely missing. Up to half of those with microphthalmia also have a syndrome that affects other organs and tissues in the body associated with the middle line disorder. They then openly discussed with us how delicate these situations can be. Many of these children end up with medical needs that can drain families financially and emotionally. They shared that, in some cases, mechanical devices are required to keep children like our son alive, and we needed to consider how we felt about our child being sustained by artificial means.

The specialists talked to us with authority, respect—and heart. Surely it was because they often dealt with similar children and their families in their work with cleft palate cases, but it was different and refreshing to have our son's condition spoken of from a compassionate, *human* perspective.

Marysol

The specialists gave us a realistic viewpoint, but unlike the previous experiences with doctors, this time I came away with a sense of peace. If God decided to allow our son to live, He would see us through. We were determined that our son would not need artificial assistance. He was going to live on his own strength. It was also encouraging to know he was otherwise healthy and strong. Hope sprang to life within me.

As we got ready to go home, we thanked the specialists for the information and for their expressions of care. This was what we'd hoped would happen with the first doctors we visited—the doctors who left us angry and disillusioned. Now we had the facts and felt equipped to go forward.

Over the next two weeks, we talked with our families about what we'd learned. Andrés finally spoke to his grandfather about our son's situation. Guillermo was worried that the baby was going to be born blind, but he never suggested abortion and was nothing but supportive. Likewise, my parents were concerned but loving, and they desired to help in any way they could. As we thought more about how difficult the birth and the days leading up to it could be, Andrés and I decided it'd be best for the child to be born in Mexico so that my parents would be available to us. A few days after that decision was made, we found out my brother Pepe had told the priests of the the *Misioneros del Espiritu Santo* about our situation. He'd also learned that the *Instituto National de Pernatologia* (INPER), a top facility for cases such as ours, was in Mexico City. Even better, the director of INPER was the cousin of father Ancona, a fellow priest of the *Misioneros del Espiritu Santo*. I was encouraged. I couldn't help but feel God was taking care of our needs.

How we managed to get to Mexico from Ecuador was also amazing, a miracle in itself—the first of many to come for us and our son.

Andrés

We picked a date to go to INPER for some initial tests, and I purchased the airline tickets. Being a Mexican citizen, Marysol didn't need a travel visa; however, Paz and I did, so we put in the request to the Mexican Embassy in Quito. We arrived there from Cuenca on a Friday morning to pick up our visas. Our flight out of Ecuador was scheduled for the very next day.

But there was a problem. When we arrived at the embassy that morning, it was closed! It was *Día de los Muertos*, a national holiday in Mexico that had completely slipped our minds. I waved down a guard and explained our dilemma. He suggested we talk to the ambassador directly and gave us directions to his residence. A short drive later, we arrived and rang the bell. No answer. With nowhere else to go and not knowing what else to do, we sat down on the sidewalk near the street, hoping someone would show up. Almost four hours later, no one had arrived. We were desperate. Norita, my mother, was with us and helping us to take care of our daughter Paz. She encouraged us to have patience and keep waiting.

Then a vehicle drove up. A man got out dressed like he was about to leave for a safari. Inside the vehicle were a woman and children. He was walking toward the entrance to the residence, documents in his hand, when he spotted us. "What are you doing here?" he inquired.

"We are waiting for the ambassador," I said. I saw him look to Marysol and notice her bulging stomach. "Our passports are at the embassy, and we need to leave tomorrow. My wife needs to give birth in Mexico."

When we gave him our names, he thought for a moment. "I don't remember seeing any passports there with those names," he said. My heart raced. It felt like it could explode any second.

"Please help us!" I pleaded.

"Wait here," he instructed. "Let me see what I can do." He entered the residence and returned ten minutes later minus the documents he was originally carrying. "Follow me!" He got into his vehicle, and we drove behind him back to the embassy. We still had no idea who he was, but he was our only hope.

We still had no idea who he was, but he was our only hope.

We were led inside the embassy and straight to his office. Shuffling through some files, he found our passports. "These never came into my hands. There are no visas." He then sat down, his hands a flurry of activity. Moments later, he handed me the required visas.

Turns out he was the consul—the only person at the embassy who could sign and approve them. We enjoyed a relieved night's sleep at our hotel and boarded our plane without incident the next day.

Marysol

We arrived in Mexico, now just one month from my due date, and headed to INPER to undergo an initial series of medical tests in preparation for the birth. Pazita stayed with my parents in a residency at the general house for the *Misioneros del Espiritu Santo*, and Andrés and I made our way to the hospital.

To get into this facility, you usually have to register three months into your pregnancy. However, thanks to father Ancona's relationship with the director, I was accepted upon arrival. The first exam was for an updated sonogram, and as we were waiting for the doctors' responses to it, I couldn't help but feel like the last thing I wanted to do was to go through another barrage of procedures. I was tired. Like any mother late in pregnancy, I simply wanted the baby to come.

Andrés

Suddenly a young doctor appeared. He strode in, hands stuffed in the pockets of his white lab coat, smugly glanced at the monitor displaying my sonogram—the living image of my son—and slapped his forehead. "Oh!" he exclaimed loudly. "This is hypoplasia of the brain!" Then he stalked out, like he was some big shot super doctor. He didn't even say, "Good evening," as he left.

Oh God, I thought. *How can he dare to say that?* I was indignant that he could just blurt out something so important and life-changing with no thought that Marysol and I were right there listening. It was so insensitive—not to mention incorrect. We'd been told hypoplasia of the eyes, a major but far less serious condition than hypoplasia of the brain. We departed into an aisle outside the sonogram room, still mad at that doctor. I was seething. "How it is possible," I asked Marysol, "for someone to be so cold? We were right there in the room!" Neither of us could fathom why they would allow such people to be doctors. Then, just as suddenly, we saw him clutch at his eye. We watched as nurses directed him into a chair. Writhing in obvious pain he was quickly surrounded by a huddle of doctors. I asked a nurse what was happening; apparently, the man's cornea had detached.

We couldn't believe it—and we decided to try to be more sensitive ourselves. We were being stretched to the edges of our endurance, and we realized it wasn't going to get any easier. Marysol endured one more procedure, an extraction of amniotic fluid from her womb, and then we met with INPER's director. We thanked him for allowing Marysol to be seen without having to register months in advance, and we set a date for the Caesarean section: December 12.

Our day at the hospital completed, we left, but my heart was heavy. I knew I couldn't stay in Mexico with Marysol and Pazita but instead had to return to Ecuador the next day. I had no choice; I couldn't afford to take time off. It was the height of the pre-holiday sales season at the jewelry store, and my grandfather needed all of his staff, especially his managers. However, I was promised time off so that I could return in time for the birth.

Marysol

As I prepared for Andrés' departure, I thought back to a dream I had earlier in my pregnancy, before we learned of Jesús' condition. I was outside our apartment building in Cuenca, standing where the cars enter the parking lot. I saw a little blonde boy sitting on the stairs. Silently, he stretched out his hand to me. Without hesitation, I took his hand in mine—and then woke up. Now, as I counted down the days to Jesús' due date, I believed that dream was my little boy's way of asking me to take him, hold on to him, and never let go.

I was determined to do just that, but I didn't want to do it alone. Ever since we were married, Andrés was always by my side, a comforting presence I could rely upon. Without him, I felt as though I was slogging through a living nightmare, a place of dark shadows where even the light was sparse and cold. My sorrow was saturated by my tears; I could not sleep. My weariness starved my thinking, while physically I felt a weight on my shoulders every bit as heavy as that of my heaving midsection. Pazita wanted me to play with her as I always had, but I couldn't. Thankfully, my parents were such an amazing, unconditional support for us, as well as my siblings, even though I was grouchy and felt completely weak with no strength to face the future. A simple smile was a task too difficult to achieve.

In the midst of this devastation, I read about the life of St. Francis of Assisi, as well as "The Silence of Mary," both books by Ignacio Larranaga. I was inspired by Francis' life and felt I was walking with Mary in the sacred season of her life when she was awaiting the birth of her Son and Lord. In these ways, God made His presence known to me in my deepest loneliness. Father Ramos and many other brothers visited from the *Misioneros del Espiritu Santo*. With him, I could talk about God and my struggle to trust in Him and not give in to the despair.

In our time apart, I spoke to Andrés by phone, and in those conversations, I felt we were close but not really together. He was so very, very far away.

Andrés

Those four weeks away from Marysol and Pazita were the most difficult of my life. I stayed busy working my leads and somehow succeeded in acquiring plenty of sales, but my head and heart were in another place—an empty, hopeless space that I was desperate to somehow fill.

A few days after my return to Ecuador, I went to the *Inmaculada Conception Cathedral* located adjacent to Calderon Park in Cuenca. Mass was underway, but I went directly to the confessional. There was no priest present, and that was fine by me, for I had no need or desire to repent of anything. I entered the dark chamber, sat, and began to weep. The sobs came, uncontrollable and relentless. My shoulders ached as my body wrenched in agony.

> I felt peace and a sense of God's presence.

"Lord," I cried, "everyone has a nose. Everyone has eyes. What will my son's life be like?" I pleaded, too, for the life of Marysol, begging God to spare her. I was in there until Mass was over—until I had no more to give. It wasn't until later that day that I realized, remarkably, that I felt peace and a sense of God's presence as a result of shouting out my greatest fears to Him. That event carried me through the remaining days of sorrow until I could finally leave Cuenca and return to my Pazita and my Marysol and get ready for the coming of our son.

Marysol

My loving parents drove Pazita and me from Querétaro to the *Misioneros del Espiritu Santo* house in Mexico City, and there we were reunited with Andrés. There were hugs, kisses, and tears, and I felt complete again with Andrés by my side. I wasn't able to allow myself to feel fully whole, though, because I knew I was about to go into the hospital to prepare for Jesús' birth the next morning. Our time together was brief yet glorious, and then Andrés took me to INPER. I was ushered into a back room and changed into a hospital gown. Then I was taken into a large area with about twenty other women—no rooms, no curtains, just beds lined up side by side. The room was full of patients, doctors, and nurses, but loneliness enveloped me like a shroud. Andrés had just arrived, and now we were separated again, and I knew I wouldn't see him until after the birth.

I was on my own; just me and Jesús.

That night was like something from a horror movie. All the women in the room were, like me, about to give birth, but they moaned and screamed with pain. All of the ladies were there because of an at-risk pregnancy. Most were young, though some were older; the woman in the bed next to me was likely in her forties. Doctors came in sporadically and unannounced, and sometimes spoke rudely to the other women. Yet when these same doctors came to my bed, I was spoken to kindly. Perhaps they thought I was related to INPER's director; I don't know. All I do know is that I was grateful I was being treated well, but I felt horribly for the other women. Surely, they had the same fears I did, wondering if their children were even going to survive the birthing process.

"Who is your doctor?" The question came from the older woman next to me.

"Doctor Ibarguengoitia," I said.

Another woman several beds away from us responded. "Oh, really? He's the best. When did you start your process to come to INPER?"

"I arrived from Ecuador," I said. "I registered about a month ago."

Despite my obvious preferential treatment in comparison to their own, no one expressed anger or bitterness toward me. I guess in that moment we were sisters; it didn't matter how or why we ended up here. We were together in this shared moment, anticipating the arrival of our children yet frightened of what could happen to them and to us.

The next day, the woman next to me had her child, and I saw her baby that night.

"Is it fine?" she asked.

I saw the baby was deep red, similar to a child born with Down's Syndrome. I looked at the woman, saw her expression of joy mixed with utter sorrow.

"Yes," I said. "It's fine."

I then turned away from her and shed my own private tears of joy—for that morning while they were doing the C-section, I suddenly found myself with a deep desire to surrender my all to God. I started to forgive and asked for forgiveness for all the people that came to mind. Then the most beautiful and powerful moment came: they showed me my son, was it was more than I could imagine. He was so beautiful, radiant, and looked so amazingly precious. Only God could do that! My hope rose! There were no complications. Jesús Andrés Malo Loyola was born December 12, 2000, at 7:47 a.m. at six pounds, six ounces. I'd been waiting for that moment, and the brilliant light of his life swept away my darkness.

Andrés

Marysol's uncle Enrique was a doctor and therefore gained access to the operating room where Jesús was born before I was allowed back. He strode into the waiting room where I was languishing, desperately awaiting news.

"He's okay, Andrés," he said. "He's an angel. You'll see."

A weight, indescribable in its bulk, lifted from my anguished soul. *He's alive*, I thought, *and she's alive!* I closed my eyes in prayer, silently pouring forth thanks to God. *I have a son.* I let out a breath like a pressure tank releasing its contents. Though her uncle hadn't said so specifically, I believed, too, that Jesús' birth was successful, and he wouldn't have to rely on artificial means to live. An hour later, I was ushered back into a room and told to put on a surgical cap, mask, gloves, and blue cloth coverings over my shoes. I passed by what I understood

> "Hola, Jesús," I said. "Cómo estás?"

to be an intensive care section, and then was led into another area where four babies lay in see-through cradles called isolettes. The nurse pointed to one, and I went forward. A round bubble like an astronaut's helmet covered the child's head and shoulders, obviously feeding oxygen to the baby. His face was easy to see, though, as was his silky blonde hair.

"Hola, Jesús," I said. "Cómo estás?"

His head turned slightly in recognition. My heart leaped. I was not yet allowed to touch him, but his response was enough. I watched him as he closed his mouth, trying to breathe through the area where his nose should be. Unable to do so, the thin skin in its place vibrated with the effort. He'd open his mouth wide to take in air and exhale. I thought he actually looked angry about the whole process. It was difficult to witness, yet it was also encouraging. In these vital minutes after his birth, Jesús was clearly learning to breathe on his own.

I was asked to leave that room, given an update on Marysol's condition, and then told I'd be allowed to see her later. I was frustrated—not for me, but for Marysol and Jesús. I didn't understand why they were separated. *A mother should be with her son.* It was so unlike the routine of Paz's birth, where she and Marysol were almost instantly reunited and I was allowed in the room to witness the birth. My patience was rewarded that afternoon, though, when I returned to see Jesús. He was in a different room with electrodes attached to his head for a hearing test. Just after I arrived, Marysol slowly walked in. "Jesús!" she said—and the boy turned his entire body toward the sound. The doctors and nurses present gasped and commented in amazement. All that mattered to me was that Jesús undeniably knew his mother's voice.

While Marysol spent the next two nights in recovery, I traveled with Jesús as he was taken back and forth by ambulance to two other hospitals, *Instituto Nacional de Pediatría* and *Hospital Ingles*, for further procedures. On the first trip, I sat in the back of the ambulance with two young nurses, a man and a woman. Jesús was in an incubator to help him breathe, and I peered out the back window as we drove along the *Periferico*, Mexico City's busiest highway. I'd been on the freeway several times in the past, but I never thought I'd be on it in an ambulance transporting my newborn son. As I looked at him and realized where I was and what I was doing, I was overwhelmed. I wept, unable to stop. The nurses simply sat in silence, in reverence for how I felt and for my unrestrained show of love for my son.

At the pediatric hospital, various tests were conducted on Jesús. He indeed had eyes behind eyelids squinted shut by the hypoplasia, but his eyeballs were no larger than one centimeter in circumference. The nasal area was studied, of course, as was his hearing and other vital functions. As tragic as all that was, I witnessed another sight almost too awful to imagine. I saw one girl there who couldn't have been more than five years of age walking with her parents; she had a tumor the size of a banana protruding outward from one of her eyelids. It was colored a deep bruising purple. I was told it was cancer. It broke my heart.

On the way back to the INPER, Jesús looked so serene and it helped the trip go faster than it seemed. I distracted myself by talking to him to see how he reacted. I covered my own nose for a long time trying to imagine how Jesús felt, for he had been breathing only by mouth for more than an entire day. I remembered times my nose was fully congested when I had the flu and how difficult it was for me to sleep because I had to keep my mouth open. Jesusito quickly became heroic to me.

At the other hospital, Jesús underwent an MRI. I watched the screen as it scanned my son's body, slice by slice, and a new concern entered my mind: *How much will all of this cost?* Jesús was receiving the best possible care available to him in Mexico, and when we first checked in to INPER before his birth, I provided my financial information and other documentation to the authorities there. We were said to be a Category Three on a scale from one to six. I still didn't know exactly what that meant, but to add to my concern about the well-being of my wife and son, the reality of the expenses of Jesús' care was just starting to hit my consciousness—and the medical care was only beginning.

Marysol

Three days after Jesús was born, I was released from INPER, and we were told he needed to be transferred to *Instituto Nacional de Pediatría* for continued treatment as soon as a space became available for him. In preparation, Andrés and I visited the floor of the pediatric hospital where Jesús would eventually be moved. There were so many babies with conditions I would've never imagined existed. We saw one infant with an abnormally bloated stomach, and another with more tubes going into her than you could count.

We also met the parents of Israel, a newborn with hydrocephalus, or "water on the brain." The child's head was huge, blown up like a balloon, and there was a tube coming from the skull to drain the fluid. We learned from his parents that he was born two months earlier and that they had visited him every day since, falling in love with their child even though they couldn't touch him. I remembered the expectant women in the large room at INPER and wondered if perhaps this mother had once been there, too. My heart ached for this couple and child.

The next day we returned and saw the same couple, crying and holding baby clothes. Israel was dead. We hugged his parents and marveled at the peace they exuded in the midst of their loss. The very space where Israel had lived and died was taken later that day by our son.

Over the next fifteen days, we learned how to feed Jesús. My breast milk was pumped daily and refrigerated, and we learned how to place the milk in a syringe at the end of a long tube that we inserted into Jesús' mouth and down his throat, deep enough to bypass the trachea and go into the esophagus so the food went into his stomach, not his lungs. He told us he was hungry by making a sucking motion with his mouth. Every morning Andrés and I went to the hospital and soon established a beloved daily routine of breakfast in the cafeteria and then time spent together with Jesús.

Andrés

We learned many other things about Jesús' condition during this time. When he was born, his testes were receded inside his body. There were no adverse effects, though, and we were told it could be surgically corrected in the future. It was also confirmed that his condition was congenital, meaning that his existing gene structure was normal. That meant that the syndrome that caused the middle section of his skull between his mouth and forehead to be underdeveloped likely occurred in the early weeks of pregnancy and could've been caused by a thousand different factors. Still, his condition was rare—so much so that he garnered a lot of attention from others in those first days of his life. Nurses and doctors alike commented on how beautiful he looked with his unusual facial appearance combined with fair, pink skin and shiny, blonde hair. Many commented that he was like a little angel, and even the priests of the *Misioneros del Espiritu Santo* insisted that babies like Jesús were angels used by God to bring their families closer to Him and His special purposes for them.

Of course, not all of the attention he received was wanted. One day as we sat in the corridor outside the viewing area where Jesús and a number of other babies were kept and treated, we were approached by a young man in a white doctor's coat. He was holding a camera. He must've been a student, and he immediately reminded me of the hot shot big mouth from a month earlier who spouted forth his misdiagnosis of hypoplasia of the brain.

"Could I take a photo of your son?" he asked.

Adrenaline surged within, and I literally felt heat rising up my body. *My son is not some guinea pig on display*, I thought. "No," I answered. My directness should have been adequate to dissuade the boy.

It wasn't. "Please, this is for a project," he said. "This is not going to be published anywhere. This will help other students learn about medicine. Your son must have a rare condition." He asked for details and I hesitantly obliged him, telling him all we had learned up to that point, but as succinctly as I could. I just wanted him to go away, and that's probably why I ultimately consented to his request. He promised he would take only one photo.

> Babies like Jesús were angels used by God to bring their families closer to Him.

I helplessly watched him through the glass as he went inside the room, positioned himself above where Jesús lay, and began clicking off shot after shot. *Chicka-chicka-chicka.* It was like he was photographing a swimsuit model.

I wanted to crush through the glass and kick him. I figured I could; after all, I knew karate. I'd then grab his camera and rip the film right out of it, exposing it to the light and ruining the pictures of Jesús and whatever else was on the roll. Next, I'd toss the camera and film on top of his prone body, and maybe give him another kick, just for good measure.

But I didn't do any of that. As I moved toward the entrance, the young man must've seen me, because he disappeared so quickly it was as though he vanished in thin air. Marysol later told me she was mad at the doctor, too, but she was actually more concerned about what I was going to do to him. Her feelings were justified. I wanted to kill the boy.

Marysol

One of the many reasons why Andrés was on edge was because in the afternoons he had to make trips to a pharmacy over an hour away to get Phenobarbital. The drug was designed to prevent babies like Jesús from having convulsions because of sleep apnea. Andrés also had to go from place to place in search of a cannula, the device needed to insert into Jesús' throat so he could have a tracheotomy, his first surgery and the one that would ensure he could continue to breathe without his mouth having to be open. The problem lies in finding a cannula that was tiny enough to fit safely in Jesús' throat. I was often overcome with anxiety and terrified with each passing day that he would stop breathing unless the cannula was found quickly.

Even more, I was scared that I wouldn't be able to meet all of Jesús' needs as a mother. I already felt like I was falling short with Paz, especially during the weeks before Jesús was born. Now I was going to have to be equal parts mother and nurse. I was desperate to get Jesús out of the hospital, but at the same time I was dreading it. I remember telling father Juan, one of the priest's brothers of the *Misioneros del Espiritu Santo*, "God chose the most incompetent woman in the world for this." The priest, who seemed to me to be secure in himself and his faith, prayed for me: "Father," he said, "grant all that I have—all of my security, all of my faith in you—to her." I appreciated his prayer, but I didn't feel like I'd necessarily been granted anything at that moment. I felt so inadequate.

Andrés

In addition to my trips to the pharmacy, Marysol and I also met with different doctors and specialists each day. Most of them gave us needed information, but they seemed insensitive to us and our plight. An exception to this treatment, however, was when we met with a social worker who was a psychologist. It was the only time we met with her, but she made a lasting impact.

"Imagine God has a huge factory filled with workers," she said. "There are people who have regular tasks, and there are other people who have more specific, difficult tasks to perform. But then, out of these thousands of people, there are maybe one or two individuals who do a very specific task, one God knows only they can achieve." She looked at me, then at Marysol. "You have been given this huge responsibility because you are special parents."

At the end of those fifteen trying days, the tracheotomy was performed, and it was a success. The next day we were allowed to take Jesús outdoors, and for the first time, he felt the touch of the wind and the warmth of the sun. It was December 30, the day we could see again our Pazita, and my parents Ita and Papón that traveled from Querétaro to México City, to celebrate New Year's Eve with the *Misioneros del Espiritu Santo*—and usher in a new year that would bring both incredible new challenges and amazing miracles.

Chapter 4

"This is mine."

Andrés

When Jesús was released from the hospital, I approached the front desk with more than just a little trepidation. The past nineteen days of constant care had required three hospitals, two ambulances, a Caesarean section, and a seemingly unending series of procedures and tests. I thought back to three years earlier, when one of my best friends gave birth prematurely in Ecuador. Thankfully, his child survived—but the bill was more than $150,000. Marysol and Jesús had perhaps required more medical care than my friend, and all I knew from signing in weeks earlier was that I was designated as a Category Three for the costs.

The receptionist processed our discharge papers and handed me the invoice. I looked at the amount. I blinked and rubbed my eyes not sure I was seeing it correctly. It was still the same. I couldn't believe it.

It was $3,000.

"Excuse me," I said, pointing to the unexpectedly low amount. "Are you sure this is correct? This includes the C-section, the hospitals, the ambulances, and all the tests?"

"Yes, sir."

"Everything?"

"Yes, sir."

Shut up, Andrés, I chided myself. *Get out while you can.* "Thank you so much!"

Thank you, God! I thought as I stepped away from the desk. *Thank you!* In the midst of my gratefulness, I again heard God say to my heart: "This is mine." I felt the same way I did back at the embassy in Ecuador when we received our visas. I sensed again that God was taking care of us, carrying us in His arms, doing the impossible for us. I still didn't know how, nor did I yet fully appreciate why He was taking care of us—but there was no doubt. God was with us.

Marysol

My breath was taken away when Andrés told me the amount of the bill. Three thousand dollars? That's all? But that *wasn't* all— because when we arrived with Jesús and Paz, who had joined us earlier that day from Querétaro, back at the *Misioneros del Espíritu Santo*, they refused to charge us anything for our long stay there. In all that time in Mexico City, we didn't have to spend money on a hotel, meals, or transportation. The priests took care of everything. In addition, they adored Jesús and make us feel as family. They saw him, his birth, and his early recovery as a miracle—quite literally. Father Ceci, knowing of the birth of our son Jesús and his condition, sent all his friends and family a Christmas card relating the birth of the Lord Jesus Christ and our Jesús, and we felt deeply moved and thankful. For the night of New Year's Eve, they held a special celebration of the Mass for us and our child, and it was wonderful; there was food, expressions of thanks, and the nuns who were so tenderhearted toward us called *Chuyito* to Jesús and that night they made fresh egg nog with real rum.

Late that night, we went to sleep in our small room in the priests' quarters. There were two twin-sized beds, one for me and Pazita, the other for Andrés, and in-between was a small table where we placed Jesús' tiny crib and mattress. Sometime in the wee hours, I heard a *thump*. I sat up and saw Andrés leap out of his bed. Jesús had fallen!

It was onto a carpet, but the drop was about three feet. Andrés picked up Jesús, and we heard the huffing noise through his open cannula that indicated he was crying, but he recovered almost instantly. The impact was cushioned because he was so thoroughly wrapped in blankets. Andrés even offered a moment of levity for Paz, who thought Jesús was hurt. "See?" he told her. "The fall knocked his nose clean off his face." What a way to ring in the New Year!

Andrés

After a refreshingly uneventful New Year's Day at the house of the *Misioneros del Espiritu Santo*, we learned that a world-renowned plastic surgeon named Fernando Ortiz Monasterio worked there, and we were fortunate to secure an appointment with him. The unique severity of Jesús' condition compelled him to meet with us, and upon arrival at his plush hotel-like offices, we were told the *maestro*, the "master," would be ready shortly. After waiting nearly an hour, we were ushered into his office, and I was struck by the man: tall, skinny, but regal, with a baritone voice and a huge nose. I immediately thought of Don Quixote, the ingenious gentleman of La Mancha. *Perhaps he'll just cut off a hunk of his nose and place it on Jesucito.* I liked him on the spot.

He was confident he could perform the surgeries—both

internally within the skull and externally where a nose would be built—within a few years. But there was a problem: we lived in Ecuador. Don Quixote gave a toothy grin. "My best disciple lives in Ecuador; Romulo Guerrero. He is excellent." He gave us Guerrero's contact information and sent us on our way.

Marysol

We drove back to Querétaro on January 4. Brothers, sisters, extended family, and even the priests who married us came by my parent's home, and Jesús was undeniably the center of attention. Paz certainly took notice of this, too. She already knew something was special about her brother, and even then, the seed was planted that would cause her to adore and fiercely defend Jesús in years to come. But that night, a sense of foreboding descended upon me. I realized that I will soon be away from my family—and my dependence upon them—and return to Ecuador where I would feel alone, without anyone other than Andrés and my Pazita. I had

> The fear of the immediate future was almost overpowering.

to be ready to take care of Jesús on my own. The mere thought brought a tingling to my chest and set me on edge. The fear of the immediate future was almost overpowering.

Andrés

Unlike Marysol, I was anxious to return to Ecuador and desperate to return to the familiarity of our Cuenca apartment. Not only did I want to have some time again with my wife and children; I wanted to settle down in our nest. We left Querétaro and journeyed back to Mexico City for our flight home. A few people looked our way as we boarded the plane and came down the aisle with our son, first aid satchel, vacuum to clean the cannula, and a small oxygen tank on a wheeled dolly. Few, though, could see his face, so no one asked any questions. I could tell Marysol was worried. I knew she was concerned about her ability to care for our son, but I was confident in her. I also had a sense that more help was on its way, though I had no idea from where.

Marysol

We flew into Quito so we could visit Andrés' family before heading home to Cuenca. The gathering was joyful and much like the one with my family in Querétaro. However, my concern about being on my own with Jesús was growing. I knew Andrés' hours would keep him away for major portions of the day: gone from 8:30 a.m. to 12:30 p.m., home for two hours (it's a Cuenca custom that lunch is always at home), and then back to work from 2:30 p.m. to 6:30 p.m. Then there was Paz; I needed to take care of her, too, and she was still a toddler.

Upon arrival in Cuenca, Andrés went right back to work—and I established a manageable routine. We started with breakfast before Andrés left for work, then I took Paz to a day care center a short walk away from our apartment and returned to care for Jesús. I fed and bathed him, leaving the cleaning of the cannula for Andrés because the process was difficult and scary for me; I always feared I was going to somehow injure Jesús. He was a quiet baby who loved bouncing in his play seat, a small, car seat-sized chair made of cloth supported by flexible rods. Before lunch, I went to get Paz and then prepared the meal. After Andrés went back to work in the early afternoon, I did what I could to play with Paz while caring for Jesús. It was difficult; I felt more like a nurse than a mother to him and quickly sensed I needed more help and more time for Paz and myself. Then came Wednesday and our weekly lunch at Grandfather Guillermo's home.

"Andrés, Marysol. I have something for you." He slid a piece a paper across the table. It had details about a local woman. "Leonor is a nurse who can come by your home every morning. She will help you with Jesús, and give you, Marysol, a chance to rest." He reached across and took my hand. "Leonor will work with you as long as you need."

I was amazed and grateful. Leonor's arrival made it possible for me to take Paz to the park on some days and also visit with Tia Marujita, Grandfather Guillermo's sister, who spoiled me with homemade breads and desserts, fresh fruit, and by being a friend I could talk to about my feelings; a gift for someone like me who is introverted. There was another woman in our apartment complex that had a daughter the same age as Paz, so we sometimes got together so they could play. It all was a welcome daily break for me from the rigors and pressures of caring for Jesús. Another breakthrough for me was when Andrés had to leave on a business trip—meaning I had to move beyond my fear of cleaning and, if needed, changing the cannula. I visited a doctor who trained me to do it successfully. This gave me confidence and allowed me to take care of the cannula when Leonor wasn't there.

Finally, we received more incredible news. As we set up our first appointment with Dr. Guerrero, we learned that his main office was in Quito, but that he travelled to Cuenca every two months to perform surgeries. Now I didn't have to worry about how we were going to get our family to and from the plastic surgery procedures. The hospital was only minutes away from our home.

I still felt overwhelmed, but not nearly as much as before. Like Andrés, I felt God was helping us in ways we could never have anticipated or make happen on our own.

Andrés

I knew that many people, from friends and coworkers to acquaintances, wanted to see Jesús, but I also knew our family needed to keep as normal a routine as possible, not only for Jesús and Paz, but for Marysol. That meant not having visitors constantly in and out at the house. Therefore, with the blessing of local priest and friend Marcelo Cevallos, we decided to have a big celebratory Mass at *Iglesia Corazon de Jesus* dedicated to Jesús our son. Against usual tradition, the priest even allowed us to be able to speak to the attendees from the pulpit. We

> While our belief in God was growing, we still had little direct knowledge of the Bible.

were delighted as over one hundred people joined us, forming a long line at the close of the service to see Jesús and embrace us. While our belief in God was growing, we still had little direct knowledge of the Bible. As we prepared the invitation cards for the mass, we noticed a passage of Scripture on the back cover of a compact disc given to us by the *Misioneros del Espiritu Santo*. It was John 9:11, a verse about a blind man appearing before the Pharisees. It read, "He answered and said, 'A Man called Jesus made clay and anointed my eyes and said to me, "Go to the pool of Siloam and wash." So I went and washed, and I received sight.'"

Because of our son's blindness, we thought it was appropriate and used it on the cards—not knowing then the added significance that verse would have on our lives a mere two years in the future.

Marysol

The first surgery performed by Dr. Guerrero took place when Jesús was one year old. The yearly procedures were designed to help the bones in the midsection of his skull grow in three different directions, making sufficient room for the air passage to the area where the nose would ultimately be placed. Dr. Guerrero's procedure was patented and proven, but it was excruciating to imagine for your child. In each surgery, screws were inserted, protruding out of the top palate in Jesús' mouth. Those screws then had to be turned a full rotation every day for two months. In another surgery, Jesús had to wear a mask fastened by bands from two metallic hooks in his mouth. For three months, it pulled his upper jaw forward. The idea was that the bones and muscles in his head would adjust and widen the air passage—but each surgery showed little progress. We were first told the surgeries would work after the first couple of years; by the sixth surgery, though, Dr. Guerrero said the procedures needed to continue until Jesús was eighteen.

That was unacceptable to us, especially since Jesús was now reacting negatively to the surgeries. He was so young for the first few surgeries, he showed no evidence of adverse reaction. By the time the final two procedures took place, though, Jesús was older and more aware of what was happening. I noticed that his learning abilities—progressing nicely through his early preschool years—began to diminish. Previously, Jesús could point to his body parts in response to hearing their name; blow a kiss or clap his feet upon verbal command; say words, heard as whispers with the cannula, but louder and clearer when the cannula opening was covered. Later, he was hesitant to do any of those things. Plus, he was angry and depressed. He pounded his fist before the surgeries; he disengaged and lay in his bed for weeks after the surgeries.

Though we were grateful for what the surgeries were trying to accomplish, Andrés and I decided it would be best for Jesús' well-being to end the surgeries when he was seven years of age.

Though we were discouraged, we again discerned God telling us, "This is mine." We were told each surgery should've cost about $18,000, but they cost only $2,500 because they were performed in Cuenca instead of in Quito. Grandfather Guillermo paid for each one in full.

In those first years, Jesús had other medical procedures, and there were times I admit feeling like my son was more of a project than a patient. We travelled to Boca Raton, Florida when Jesús was four years of age for a treatment to expand his eyelids and help the eye sockets to grow.

A more routine procedure was done when Jesús was four to release the testes from inside his body. It brought some good news: his testes were fully functional, so someday Jesús can be a father.

Andrés

It was during these early years of Jesús' life that Marysol and I began to see the uplifting influence our son had on the lives of others. In Hispanic culture, people with disabilities are generally kept inside and out of the public eye. Some people are uncomfortable with how to respond to someone with a physical impairment; others are simply ignorant or feel uncomfortable about those with disabilities. At least that's the case with adults; however, children are not yet jaded by such perceptions or concerns. We made it a habit to take Jesús outside in public as often as possible. I often wore one of those harnesses designed to carry babies around like they were in a backpack, but I'd keep Jesús facing outward so that he was seen. Children always approached and asked the expected, unfiltered questions: "Where are his eyes?" "Where is his nose?" Then they said hello, and Jesús usually reached out his hand to them. They loved it—and even more important, I know Jesús did, too. Then some adults ventured forth, and many who told us how his face and smile touched their heart.

Jesús has a presence about him. There were many instances where Jesús would make Marysol and I feel peaceful when we were anything but at peace. My grandmother Alicia, "Mama Shisha," once dreamed that she saw Jesús with his eyes fully intact; she said, "Christ is going to give His own eyes to my great grandson Jesús." She also said she prayed twice as often for Jesús. In the three years before he passed away, grandfather Guillermo would often close his eyes for hours at a time. He wasn't sleeping; perhaps he was daydreaming or praying, I don't know. But whenever I asked, he said he was closing his eyes for Jesucito. Other family members shared that their faith in God had increased because of Jesús.

Of course, there were people who reacted negatively when they saw Jesús, and if Paz was with us when it happened, she became quite angry. It's too bad she wasn't around when the vacuum needed to clean Jesús' cannula was stolen. It was taken from inside my car along with my blue coat. That afternoon I created and printed copies of sheets and distributed them all over Cuenca, especially in the market areas where I knew the machine might be sold. The sheets included a photo of the vacuum and an explanation of why the machine was vital to my son's life. I added, "You won't be able to sell it. Please keep the coat, but I need the machine." I promised a reward and ended with my phone number. While the machine was missing, we painstakingly cleaned the cannula manually and hoped for a response. Two days later, a

> Family members shared that their faith in God had increased because of Jesús.

person stopped by my office. He had the machine and requested the reward. I pulled out fifty dollars.

"I could've sold it for more," the man said. I had no idea if he was the thief or a friend of the thief. Nor did I care. I set down the cash. "This is it. Take it or leave it." He took it, and I gratefully took the vacuum home to a much more grateful Marysol.

Marysol

Another significant moment in the first year of Jesús' life was something we certainly didn't expect, nor did we plan. When Jesús was just eight months old, my brother Pepe visited us in Ecuador, and his arrival couldn't have been more perfectly timed. Before then, I'd never been able to find the same type of spiritual support and community in Cuenca that I was used to in Mexico and I felt very lonely and with no spiritual support. Back home, I was part of *El Apostolado de la Cruz,* one of the ministries of the *Misioneros del Espiritu Santo,* where I was nurtured and was an active part of a vibrant community of faith called *Santa Bárbara.* In Cuenca, father Marcelo was close to us, and he was very kind inviting us to be part of the parish activities, but it wasn't the same and was ultimately unfulfilling. Because Pepe was a priest, he was able to bring me some spiritual refreshment.

As part of our time together, we went to Casa Blanca beach in northern Ecuador. Though our nurse accompanied us, I still wasn't feeling confident about myself or how effectively I was dealing with Jesús and his condition. Pepe offered words and prayers of comfort that I desperately needed.

On the way back home from that beach, I suddenly felt ill. I threw up. I *never* threw up, unless—

I was pregnant.

Andrés, Marysol, and Paz in Cuenca, Ecuador, 1999.

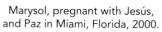

Marysol, pregnant with Jesús, and Paz in Miami, Florida, 2000.

Andrés, Marysol, and Paz.

Andrés and Paz in Cuenca, Ecuador, 1999.

When Andrés & Marysol first met. Querétaro, Mexico, Summer 1989.

Herón 'Papón', Aidita, Pepe, Marysol and Andrés
in Querétaro, México, Summer 1996.

"Entonces qué, Malo?" Andres & Marysol at Caffé Tulip,
Querétaro, Mexico, Summer 1996.

Marysol visiting Cuenca,
Ecuador, Winter 1996.

Caridad, Paty, Andrés, Marysol, Norita, Aidita,
Herón, Chiqui, Guillermo.

Engagement Ring,
Querétaro, Mexico, 1997.

Wedding, Querétaro, Mexico,
January 3, 1998.

Second wedding reception in
Cuenca, Ecuador, Uzhupud, 1998.

Jesús first picture with Andrés & Marysol,
just dismissed from the hospital, December 30, 2000.

Jesús' baptism, January 2001, *Misioneros Del Espiritu Santo*,
Santa Bárbara, Querétaro, Mexico.

With Great Grandma Alicia *"Mama Shisha,"* Cuenca, Ecuador, 2001.

Paz and Jesús at our apartment after his first surgery,
Cuenca, Ecuador, Winter 2001.

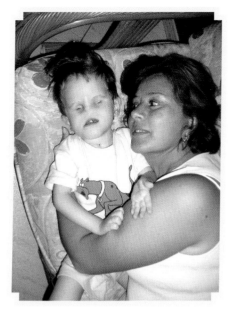

With Grandma Norita
Esmeraldas, December 2004.

Sofi, Jesús, Paz, Marysol and Andrés
The "I want one for Christmas!" day.
Parque La Carolina, Quito

"My first bath tub." Cuenca, Ecuador, 2001.

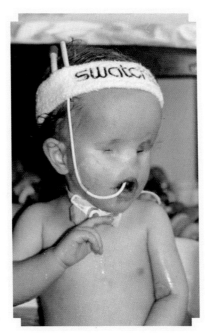

After first surgery in Cuenca,
Ecuador, Winter 2001.

22 years later.
Remembering the
unforgettable touch of
God in May 1989. Photo
at San Carlos, Mexico.

Paz, Marysol, Jesús, Andrés, and Sofi
Vacations at San Carlos, Sonora
México Feb 2011

Sofi comes into the family April 4, 2002. Cuenca, Ecuador.

Jesús getting to know his new baby sister, Cuenca, Ecuador, Spring 2002.

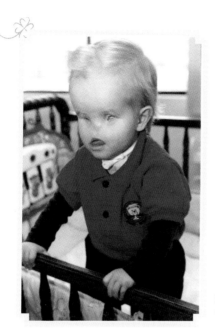

September 2001,
Cuenca, Ecuador.

Malo Loyola Family, weeks before moving to our first owned home.
September 2002, Cuenca, Ecuador.

Mother and son at *Instituto Especial de Invidentes y Sordos del Azuay*, Cuenca, Ecuador, 2003.

Mall Del Rio, Cuenca, Ecuador, 2004.

Paz with Great Grandpa Guillermo
Cuenca, 2005

Jesús' sixth surgery, Cuenca, Ecuador, 2006.
A good man leaves an inheritance to his children's children.
Pro 13:22

50 day trip to Fort Lauderdale
for Jesús' ocularist treatment,
Florida, Spring 2006.

Fort Lauderdale, Florida, Spring 2006.

Fort Lauderdale, Florida, Spring 2006.

"Mom stretching the girls,"
Fort Lauderdale, Florida,
Spring 2006.

Brother Saúl, Guillermo and Milagros Aguayo, Jimmy and Aida Cornejo, Craig and Jan Hill, Andrés and Marysol Malo.

MannaRelief Convention: Sam and Linda Caster, Founders of Mannatech and MannaRelief Ministries. Thanks to 5+ years of MannaRelief donations to FAICE, the lives of many blind children were improved. Dallas, Texas, 2007.

Receiving a donation from MannaRelief for FAICE – Ecuadorian Foundation For The Blind. Paul and Lorena Moreno, teacher Fernanda Sánchez, Marysol, Jesús, Andrés, a music teacher, Cuenca, Ecuador, 2007.

Valerie Moser (Miami Lighthouse For The Blind) and Marysol Malo (FAICE) during Seminar for Special Education for the Blind. Cuenca, June 2017

Tucson FFI Team – Floyd Residence. Standing: Jim and Jan McSheffrey, Ben Cromey, Karen Cromey, Edie Hurley, Randy Ford, Doug Cromey, Annie. Seated: Jim and Linda Floyd, Libby Ford, Andrés and Marysol, and Jesús.

With Dennis Mutchler and Judy Rubin, Arizona, 2008.

Jesús arriving from ASDB,
Tucson, Arizona, 2009.

ASDB: Jesús, Tucson,
Arizona, 2011.

With Steve Shermet, Tucson, Arizona, 2011

Debi Resner and Jesús at
Beth Sar Shalom. Tucson,
Arizona, 2011.

Jesús at ASDB, Tucson, Arizona, 2011.

ASDB: Jesús, Tucson, Arizona.

Jesús at Therapeutic Riding of Tucson, Tucson, Arizona, 2012.

Everyone hugging *Nessy*
November 2011, Tucson, Arizona.

Jesús and Sofi at the Park
Tucson, Arizona, 2014.

At Doolen Middle School with Ms. Lisa Benington Sky
and her special education team.

Mothers Day,
Tucson, Arizona, 2014.

Mothers Day,
Tucson, Arizona, 2014.

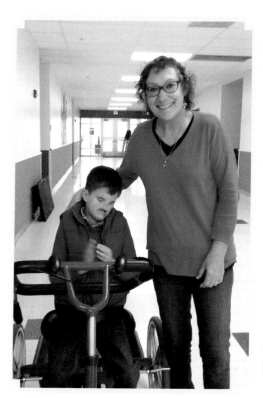

With Mrs. Linda Patten
at Cienega High School,
Vail, Arizona.

Cienega High School
2017's Year Book

Our Ecuadorian family, vacations at Esmeraldas, Ecuador, 2005.

Our Mexican family, vacation at Valle De Bravo, México, 2016.

Covenant Marriage Course, *Centro Cristiano Carismático*,
Tucson, Arizona, Summer 2018.

Presenting KickStarter campaign book update, Tucson, Arizona, 2018.

TrebolDe4.com. A Four-Leaf Clover plate design.

We chose this design because of the dreams that the Lord gave us about Jesucito. Two Bible verses inspired this design:

Hebrews 11:1, "Now faith is the substance of things hoped for, the evidence of things not seen," and Isaiah 42:9, "Behold, the former things have come to pass, And new things I declare; Before they spring forth I tell you of them."

The Lord announcing the things He will do before they occur, such as the dreams.

Chapter 5

"If you really exist, show me."

Marysol

After returning home from the beach, I took an at-home pregnancy test and then went to the doctor. It was confirmed. I was going to have another baby.

At first, I was mad at Andrés; we didn't like using contraception, and we had agreed he would take the responsibility of knowing when we were able to be sexually active each month to avoid pregnancy. As the reality set in, though, that anger faded and was replaced by a mix of emotions. I was happy but in shock; excited but frightened; looking forward to the arrival of our third child, yet questioning, *How am I going to take care of another baby?* Even worse, *Will something be wrong with this child?*

I found myself reverting back to past insecurities. "Why me, God?" I pleaded. "I am so incapable." I wanted to curl myself into a tiny ball and roll into the safety and comfort of Andrés' arms— to melt away and let him take care of me and of everything. I felt broken, not because I didn't want another child, but because of all the responsibility and worries about what was going to happen next.

Another ongoing struggle was reaching its peak. Ever since moving to Ecuador after marrying Andrés, I'd felt out of place. In Mexico, I was very close to my family, especially my mother. I'd been that way since I was a little girl. Friends or cousins asked me to sleepovers at their homes, and I always refused because I loved being at home. As the youngest of five children, my home was a place of security. I'd rather be there than anywhere else. When I met and fell in love with Andrés, I desired to be with him, but because of the on again-off again nature of our early relationship, it wasn't until after we were married that we finally had a chance get to spend time together, one-on-one, and enjoy each other as a newlywed couple. But when we moved from Mexico to Ecuador, I wasn't ready for the change. The expectations for what a woman should be in that culture are so different. In Mexico, my mother doted over us, and we had maids as well, so I wasn't required to tend to household chores, cooking, and other tasks that would've better prepared me to be a wife and mother. In Cuenca, I felt I should instantly settle down, settle in, become *Señora de Malo,* and go about my day more like an old woman instead of the inexperienced bride that I was. Plus, Cuenca is a much smaller city than Querétaro, and Andrés' family was well known in the city; this placed unintended pressure on me to conform quickly to Ecuadorian ways. Finally, we started our family right away; I became pregnant with Paz about six months after we moved to Cuenca. Then came the pregnancy with Jesús and his unique challenges—and now I was pregnant again, three in a row!

Andrés

By the time Marysol became pregnant in July 2001, we were also having problems relating to each other as a couple. Our commitment to one another was unquestioned, but we sometimes had trouble interacting without causing offense. I remember one time I came home for lunch, opened the refrigerator to get some juice, and saw that Marysol had made a special dessert. I was excited and pleased, but I didn't say anything, not wanting to spoil the surprise of having it presented after the meal. Twenty minutes later, lunch was finished but there was no dessert. I asked Marysol about it, and she had given it to Tia Marujita. "Why?" I asked. She retorted, "Because you didn't say anything when you saw it in the refrigerator, and I thought you didn't like it."

It sounds petty, but it really wasn't; the pressures of being newlyweds and young parents, coupled with the added challenges brought on by Jesús and his condition, were taking their toll. On top of that, we were struggling to find other people who could identify with us. In Cuenca, we felt like some of our social gatherings were superficial. A typical party finds the women clustered in one corner of the room while the men meet in

> We loved each other and our children, but we discerned we needed something more.

another area. We were not used to it, and it was awkward for us. So, a few months after the pregnancy was confirmed, we asked God to send us couples with whom we could relate, befriend— and who could help us draw closer to each other and perhaps even deepen our fledgling faith. Our shared care for Paz and Jesús bonded us, and we loved each other and our children, but we discerned we needed something more.

The following week, John Saavedra, a colleague who worked near me downtown for a financial company, told me about a men's Bible study every Friday morning at the home of a gentleman named Eduardo Gonzales. When I arrived there, the smell of fresh coffee and the aromatic breads and cheeses of Cuenca invited me in—and I sensed, for the first time since I was eighteen, a stirring within my spirit. That was when I was in college in Guaymas before I met Marysol and was in the darkest days of my young life. Two pivotal events had just happened back home in Ecuador: I learned that one of my best childhood friends had committed suicide, and at the same time had discovered my mother, divorced from my father just a year earlier, was seeing another man. My friend, and my hopes for reconciliation for my parents, was killed, both in the same week. I walked the campus less like a student and more like a zombie, smelling the fresh air from the nearby *Mar De Cortéz* at the Gulf of California, but incapable of being revitalized by it. *I am crushed,* I thought as I trudged to the next class. *My life has no meaning.*

Enter Delfino Cuauhtemoc, a skinny, dark-skinned Mexican classmate with a huge afro like the character El Tibiri Tabara from *Los Polivoces,* and he had a peculiar demeanor. Delfino greeted everyone with a handshake and the words, "Hi, I'm Delfino. Jesus loves you and I love you." He was a smart student, and I used to tease him by coming up behind him, blowing cigarette smoke into the back of his afro, and then watching the smoke slowly waft upward from the big, black curls. I told him he was so smart his brain was on fire. He put up with the prank, until one day he turned around to face me, his face a perfect picture of serenity, his voice calm.

"Andrés. How are you doing?" He paused. "Why are you bothering me?"

I explained the joke in defense of my action, though he surely already knew why I was doing it. Then he said, "I'd like you to go to church with me. This weekend." Something within my hurting heart leaped at his unexpected response. "Sure. I'll go."

We went in my car to Empalme, a poverty-stricken town located across the bay just east of Guaymas. I was amazed at what I saw: the church floor was dirt, and the church, if you could call it that, consisted of wooden poles with a tarp for a roof. Yet the people were not only happy, they were filled with joy and passionately praying and worshipping. I'd never seen anything like it. Near the close of the service, we were asked to hold hands and pray, a first for me. Everyone else was praying aloud with their eyes closed, but mine were wide open. Then the girl next to me, a perfect stranger, starts to cry. "Oh, Lord," she said, "I can sense the heart of Andrés and how much he is suffering." It was incredible, but I couldn't feel anything my emotions were so drained. Afterward, me, Delfino, and others from the church were invited to a woman's house. It was more of a shack, but she happily offered us tortillas; the only food she had. She told us that she had seven children, each with stories more tragic than the other. I asked her how much she spent each week, and when she said twenty pesos I was surprised because that was how much I spent on a single outing to eat with my friends. What struck me most was her peace and her happy face when she told those stories of her life, but her deep black eyes and white teeth were overflowing with joy to the point that it made me feel uncomfortable.

On the drive back to Guaymas, where I was to drop off Delfino before proceeding to my apartment just down the highway in San Carlos, I told him, "This isn't for me. I'm not the type of person to go door to door with a Bible."

He smiled. "No one is asking you to do that. I don't do that.

But God has thousands of ways to invite you to let Him into your heart, but He won't come in without your consent."

In the weeks to come, I spent more time with Delfino, and we had more conversations about spirituality. Once I told him about a book I was reading sent to me by my uncle: *The Autobiography of a Yogi* by Paramahansa Yogananda. Again, Delfino was kind, non-judgmental, but direct. He told me about the church in Leodicea from the book of Revelation. "You cannot be lukewarm, Andrés, with one foot in Jesus and the other in the yogi," he said. "But Jesus stands at the door of your heart and is knocking. If you will hear His voice and open the door, He will come in and eat with you, and you with Him. Jesus will clean your heart."

For whatever reason, Delfino's words touched me. *God can clean my heart?* In my despair, I knew I wanted to be clean. *I wonder if this is real?*

Near the end of the semester in May, Delfino and I were returning from the church in Empalme when I felt compelled to go to a Catholic church. To my surprise, he agreed to join me. We found the main cathedral in Guaymas and walked up to the front doors. The church was closed. Delfino sensed the moment; we went to our knees in prayer, and he placed his hands on my head, and asked me to repeat a prayer asking Jesus Christ to come into my heart. As we prayed, I heard people from the park, undoubtedly drunk, yelling and teasing us, calling us sissies and words far worse—but I didn't care. I wanted to invite Jesus in. Yet even then, there was doubt. After taking Delfino home that evening, I stopped on the highway outside San Carlos, parked, and hiked up a desert hill adjacent to the road. There was a water reservoir at the summit. I stood beside it and looked up at the stars piercing the cloudless sky. "God," I said. "If you really exist, show me." I continued, "God, I don't believe my friend Hernan committed suicide in his right mind. I really think it was an accident. Please forgive him." My head was swimming at what I was saying, but I was desperate to hear from God. "Lord," I said, "my life makes no sense."

When I came down the hill, two police officers were parked behind my car. Drug use and trade was common there, and they wanted to know what I was doing on that hill at night. "I was praying," I said, and then quoted the familiar "Our Father, who art in Heaven…" prayer to help them understand what I was doing. After a couple more questions, I showed them my student ID and they were convinced I wasn't involved in wrongdoing and left me to drive to my apartment five minutes away. My roommate Fausto was elsewhere partying true to his saying, "To drink 'til dawn." I was exhausted anyway and I fell asleep.

Next thing I remember I had the most vivid dream, clearer than any I had ever experienced. In it I saw the face of Delfino. "Hit your past, Andrés," he said. Then he made a gesture with his hand and an image of Delfino's face from before He knew Jesus appeared above the one that spoke to me. Then I made the same gesture with my hand to "hit" my own past and heard Delfino's unmistakably contagious laughter. Next, an intense light appeared to my right. I knew I was still dreaming but did not want to open my eyes, for the presence that came with that light caused a joy so intense that it had a sense of supernatural love with power without limitation. I felt a vibration, *bzzzz*, inside my chest. It was completely audible, visible, palpable, and inexplicable!

I recalled at that moment what I had asked God the night before, for a sign of his existence, and believed He was visiting me with this incredible dream that was becoming a happy reality. When I opened my eyes, I still felt the vibration in my chest, and

God brought a vision to my soul, of myself as a baby in the arms of Christ.

"Thank you, God! Thank you, God!" I wept with joy. I knew the Lord had forgiven my sin. I woke up lying on my left side to realize the sun was just coming up. It must've been 5:00 in the morning. I kept crying and saying, "Thank you, God! Thank you, God! Thank you, God!"

From my bed in front of the window, I saw the bay and on the other side, at the top of the mountains, the sunlight began to shine on the horizon. I knew that light was the Lord Jesus! I continued feeling that delicious joy in my chest, the *bzzzz* that made me cry indescribable joy because God had answered me! I got up, went outside, and walked toward the rocks at the edge of the bay. I watched the sunrise, still crying, still laughing, still unable to stop saying "Thank you, God!" I rejoiced there for about twenty minutes or so.

> "Thank you, God! Thank you, God!" I wept with joy.

And I knew.

God was real!

The following month was the beginning of my summer in Querétaro where I met Marysol. When I returned to Guaymas in the fall, I continued my friendship with Delfino. I went to church services with him a few times, once to a Sunday gathering in a local theater, and I often asked him questions about God. I was hungry to know more—but no one, including Delfino, told me I needed to get a Bible or go to church. At the start of the new year, my studies ended in Guaymas and I returned to Querétaro, but I couldn't find any other churches there except Catholic parishes. There was nothing comparable to what I saw in Empalme, and I longed to have the same experience as the one in San Carlos.

Ultimately, I attended a Kung Fu class in Querétaro, which redirected my spiritual journey away from Christianity. Later, during two-plus years in Mexico City, I deepened my search—delving into everything from meditation and Buddhism, to a study of Chakras from Hinduism and yoga, to Krishna Consciousness. Everything left me empty and unfulfilled. I knew there was something more.

Now, here I was in Cuenca at this study with five other men, and they were using a book by T.D. Jakes called *Hombre, Eres Libre* ("Loose That Man and Let Him Go!") with this book at this study, the faith of my youth was revived within. It was delicious spiritual food that my soul was starving to receive, and while I struggled to get up early most mornings, I couldn't wait to rise with the sun every Friday and get over the Eduardo Gonzales' home. We'd read, Eduardo would teach a principle of Scripture, and then we'd discuss it. As I started reading the Bible for myself for the first time, it simply came alive. As I continued to attend the studies, I knew I'd come out of my spiritual desert. I had found what was real—again. My heart could only repeat "Thank you God!"

Marysol

The same week Andrés was invited to attend the Friday morning men's group, Paola Robalino, Jesús's therapist, invited me to a prayer group. The following afternoon, a friend in our apartment building, Marcela Herrera, asked me if I'd like to return with her to a different prayer meeting at the home of Alejandra Gonzales. I found the first visit uninteresting and expected it to be the same, but I said I'd go. It turns out it was being led by Ximena, Eduardo Gonzales' wife. When I walked in, other ladies were sitting in the family room on couches, and tea was being served. It was comfortable for me and I felt welcome. They were reading from *Becoming a Woman of Freedom* by Cynthia Heald, and the book told what the Bible said about being a wife, mother, and a woman of God. I never knew the Bible talked about those things. It was beautiful for me to see that God had a plan in His Word that provided the answers I needed for what I was experiencing in my life at that time. Then one of the ladies shared with me that the Bible they were using was the same one I used as a Catholic. This shocked me; I always understood that Protestants were a sect of some kind. I left with a sense of excitement and joy, but also one of concern that, as a Catholic, I'd somehow done something wrong to not only study with these people—but enjoy it.

The next day, I called my brother Pepe. As the phone rang, I remembered telling him in the past that I wanted to try to read the Bible, and how he had advised me to start with the book of John. A couple of times I tried to read, but it was hard to understand. Now, at this study, it seemed the Bible was speaking directly to my heart, and I wasn't sure how to handle it.

"I went to this group," I said to Pepe. "They were reading the Bible, and it was the same Bible that Catholics use."

I'm sure he could hear the unease in my voice. "How did you feel?"

"I felt really good."

He paused. "Okay, Mary," he said, using the diminutive of my name, tenderly. "Go ahead."

I was a proud Catholic; I had no reason not to be. Catholicism introduced me to a God and His Son who loved me, and to a faith I treasured from childhood. To receive Pepe's affirmation was reassuring. As the studies continued, there were times I was offended when Catholicism was criticized and sometimes even ridiculed. I didn't like it at all: I was a Catholic, but I was also a Christian—I believed that with all my heart. Yet I continued to learn more about the Bible and what God's Word had to say to me as a woman, and it was exhilarating. It was also preparing me for a later moment of divine confrontation that would change my life even more.

> I continued to learn more about the Bible and what God's Word had to say to me as a woman.

Andrés

Our original prayer, of course, was for God to send us couples, and Eduardo and Ximena quickly became friends and mentors to us. They also introduced us to Sonia and Diego Pesantes. Through these couples, especially Eduardo and Ximena, we were encouraged to learn more about Jesús and the Bible. I was inspired as I discovered through them that marriage is God's idea, a reflection of His relationship with other Christians as His "bride," and I watched as Eduardo and Ximena lived out that husband-wife relationship before me and Marysol. It was weird for me to see Eduardo still be happy even though he wasn't smoking or drinking, two commonplace habits that were just a part of what most men were in Cuenca. I also noticed how Eduardo and Diego always talked positively about their wives in private and in public. It was a model to me of how to be a Christian husband and man.

Marysol

The couples helped me to learn that the source of my security and happiness was not to come from my husband, but from Jesus. Ximena, especially, shared how she had come out from severe difficulty in the past. Her vulnerability allowed me to feel more comfortable with dealing with, and sometimes sharing, my vulnerabilities—particularly my fears about being a mother and a woman in Cuenca culture. I saw, too, how Eduardo and Diego were not afraid to say, "I love Jesus" and tell others how He was the reason their marriages were so strong, and I began to see how this had a wonderful effect on Andrés. Even though both men were from established families in Cuenca, they were bold and unwavering about their faith in God. As a result of all this influence from these couples, Andrés and I developed a better understanding of each other and our communication with one another improved.

This interaction with the couples continued into early 2002 as my pregnancy progressed and we learned that we were going to have a second girl. Hope and joy grew within me, and I became less fretful and more excited about the pending birth. The women even prayed over my unborn child and blessed her. The ladies gave me some ideas for her name, and Andrés and I ultimately chose Maria Sofia because it meant that she had a destiny from God to be a woman of wisdom. Then Eduardo and Ximena invited Andrés and me to attend an overnight retreat about a half-hour drive outside Cuenca in the mountain town of Paute. Even though it was going to take place in March, just one month before Sofi's due date, we decided to attend. It would be the first time since Jesús' birth that I'd be apart from him for longer than a day. We made our plans for Andrés' grandmother, Alicia, or "Mama Shisha," to stay at our home with the children while we were away, and Jesús' nurse agreed to stay overnight as well.

The retreat started on a Friday evening, and then continued throughout the next day before we returned to Cuenca Saturday night. Women travelled together in one set of buses, the men in another, and sleeping arrangements were also segregated, even for married couples. I'd only be able to visit with Andrés during breaks and right before bedtime Friday. As a Catholic in Mexico, I loved going to retreats from the time I was a little girl. But I knew that this was a Protestant retreat, so I was a little nervous yet strangely excited about what was going to happen. Friday night I was alone in my group with Ximena and one other attendee. There was no teaching that night, only singing and prayer. The chorus of one song penetrated my heart. It said, "It's difficult to believe, Lord, but I will wait patiently on you." The words spoke to my remaining concerns about the pressures of my life as a wife and mother, as well as to the internal struggle going on within me as my Catholic traditions conflicted with this new, different Protestant experience. I slept peacefully and woke up the next morning thinking of something else I'd heard the night before: "From the fruit of your lips you will reap." All day Saturday found me surrounded by loving women and hearing teaching on children, marriage, and how to be a woman of faith. Women were preaching, too, and they were empowered; it was something I'd never seen before. It was like I was a baby bird in a warm nest. I felt nurtured and safe.

Andrés

At the retreat, I was with a group of men similar in age to me. When we arrived at our classroom on Friday, there was a painting on the wall of Jesus tending a flock of sheep. It was serene and gave me a sense of peace. We worshipped, singing one song after another, and my spirit leaped within. It was the first time since those dusty outdoor services with Delfino in Empalme that I had seen worship like this. I closed my eyes, heard the voices of other men singing praise to God, and I was breathless. I felt like I was returning to an eternal home. The old vibration on my chest *bzzzz* recalled my first experience with God in San Carlos. Tears streamed down my face. My heartbeat drummed in my chest, and again there was that vibrating "sound" of joy as warmth cascaded from my chest and spread all over my body. It was glorious!

> I felt like I was returning to an eternal home.

The next day, we were taught about the parable of the Prodigal Son, and then we put together a play about the story. I was randomly chosen by the men for the role of the prodigal, and as I portrayed the part, I exulted within at how the son's journey mirrored my own. It was significant, and it was also fun: I made the other men laugh as I helped them get into character as pigs under my care. As we got ready to board the buses to return to Cuenca, my joy was so complete I didn't have a care in the world. As we reached the end of the trip about 7:00 p.m. and I saw where the buses were taking us, I laughed out loud. We were pulling up to a street next to a church. When Marysol and I used to drive past the church, *Centro Cristiano de Cuenca*, I used to tease, "That's where all the 'Crazy Hallelujahs' go to church." It was pastored by Jimmy and Aída Cornejo, a couple Marysol and I met at the retreat.

Now it was exactly where we were going for a post-retreat service. I couldn't wait to get inside.

Marysol

I was anything but excited when our bus arrived. The men had got there first, and I remembered the church, and what Andrés and I used to say about it, immediately upon sight. As I departed the bus, I rubbed my hand through my hair and looked down at the pavement, my actions mirroring the reinvigorated conflict within. I found Andrés inside and was instantly annoyed at how ridiculously happy he looked. We didn't take a seat; songs of worship were already underway. We stood, and I watched others clapping or raising their hands as they sang. I was equal parts afraid and enthralled. No one spoke, but ultimately someone announced that people could get baptized if they wanted. Andrés was ready to get immersed on the spot and asked if I wanted to join him. "No," I responded. "Go by yourself." He chose to wait. As the service wound down, I couldn't wait to leave. It's true I was anxious to see Jesús and Paz, but I was also ready for this wonderful but weird getaway to end.

Weeks later, we were back at the "Crazy Hallelujahs" church with the kids attending my first official Protestant church service. Eduardo and Ximena sat with us, and he couldn't help but notice how I was standing still, arms folded across my chest, while everyone else was singing or dancing or speaking in another language that I was told was called "tongues."

Eduardo leaned across to me. "Marysol. Soon I will see you dancing and worshipping, too."

"You're crazy!" I said, perhaps a little more aggressively than intended. He just smiled and renewed his singing.

From then on, we went to church at *Centro Cristiano de Cuenca* Every Thursday and Sunday, while I went alone to Catholic Mass every Monday. This made my conflict external as well as internal. I'd already realized Catholic services in Cuenca were different than those I'd attended with the *Misioneros del Espiritu Santo*. What was happening to me?

My question was put on hold by the birth of Sofi. My parents and mother-in-law arrived after the birth, but Ximena visited to pray with me before I went into labor, and both Eduardo and Ximena returned to see Andrés and I after her birth. Back when Paz was born, my labor was difficult and resulted in a C-section, as was the case for Jesús, so the doctors agreed I'd have a third C-section for Sofi's birth.

Everything went perfectly and, unlike Paz and Jesús, Sofi came out of my womb ready to eat. In the days that followed, she strengthened quickly and slept peacefully. Even more, I went through a season of healing and restoration, and Sofi was God's gift to me after having such a traumatic pregnancy and birth with Jesús just sixteen months earlier. After Sofi's birth, Andrés and I embraced a sense of optimism about the future, even as we continued caring for Jesús and Paz.

Little did we know that God was about to birth something else in our lives—inspired by Jesús—that was going to touch the lives of blind people all over Cuenca.

Andrés

About a year after attending *Centro Cristiano de Cuenca*, we attended a Thursday evening service featuring a preacher with the gift of miracles. He spoke for an hour, then called people who wanted to be healed to come forward. Many people responded, including a girl who had already had five different surgeries on her left leg. The preacher asked the rest of the congregation to come closer, saying he wanted us to witness what God was about to do.

Marysol and I approached along with about a hundred other people, and we got as close to the pulpit as we could. The preacher seated the girl in a chair and asked for a doctor from the crowd. When the doctor arrived, he was asked to state his name and his specialty, and then the preacher confirmed with the crowd that the doctor was a recognized physician in the city. Next, the preacher asked the girl to announce into the microphone the condition of her left leg and to explain what had been done in the surgeries. Her left leg was clearly shorter than the right, probably by about ten centimeters or so. We could all see that the girl's hips were firmly against the back of the chair, and that both of her legs were extended out straight. The size difference was clearly visible.

Then the speaker asked someone else to hold the microphone close to his mouth as he leaned over and put both hands under the girl's legs. *This one has to be an extraordinary magician to get out of here alive*, I thought amusingly to myself. But what happened in the next ten seconds was completely supernatural! After the doctor had felt both legs of the girl and nodded that they were her actual legs, the audience listened in silence as the preacher prayed—then were stunned as the left leg of the girl stretched to match the length of the right leg. Cries of all kinds were heard throughout the crowd as well as weeping. Some were euphoric, others screamed with fear. I began trembling and started to cry as I watched the face of the girl transform from frightened cries to an expression of utter joy! I was shaking so hard it hurt, but I was trying to control my body. "What the heck!" I said to Marysol. "God! Did you see that? What is this! How incredible!"

Over the next ten minutes, others in the room began rejoicing, saying they, too, had been physically healed. They included our good friend Pablo Pesantes, who shouted with joy as he took off and on his eyeglasses. "My eyes!" he cried. "I

> The left leg of the girl stretched to match the length of the right leg.

do not need my glasses! I see blurred with them on! Thank you, my God!" Another person, an old, indigenous woman wearing a skirt typical of the women of the towns surrounding Cuenca, cried out, "My God! Lord, my God!" She had been blind for several years and now declared that she could see perfectly! Her son was with her and confirmed what she said. *She cannot be lying*, I thought, in that she had all the characteristics of an honest and good woman, one who was fearful of playing with the things of God.

It was a completely new experience, one that penetrated my whole being. One thought stayed with me. *All this is really happening!* The thought of that made my body shake violently, something that was completely new, too. God had moved powerfully in our midst!

Chapter 6

"Do you have the Life?"

Andrés

Being a father is such a joy! When Paz was born, I experienced all the "firsts" of being a Daddy—from diaper changes and first steps to bedtime stories and first words. With Jesús, there were other "firsts" resulting from his condition: cleaning the cannula, learning how he communicates, and dealing with his blindness. Of course, there was also the pride of having a boy, a son, upon whom I could impart my experiences as a man.

Yet Sofi brought new "firsts" that I didn't anticipate. Her mere presence had such a positive impact on the other children. Her cries as an infant were new to Jesús and brought out such tenderness from him. He'd gently stroke her hands and face, grinning as she quieted under his touch. Because she and Jesús were so close in age, Paz became more than a big sister to her and her brother; she was a miniature Mommy. Marysol marveled at how secure Paz was as she helped feed, clothe, and care for her siblings. As I watched my little trio interact with each other, and witnessed the ways they uplifted Marysol, warmth spread throughout my body and into my heart and soul. I grew more confident and content as my family fulfilled me.

But with this sense of assurance also came a realization that Jesús' medical needs required special attention that I wasn't certain could be met in Cuenca. With a population of 300,000, Cuenca wasn't a small town, but it wasn't a large city, either. It evidently had its share of blind people, though. There was a young blind woman who sold candy in the streets, and I observed how she handled the candies and coins and could with her touch tell the difference between the different confections and currencies. I knew another blind man, Miguel, who sold candles outside the city's emblematic cathedral, and I watched how he successfully walked from place to place and rode the bus back and forth each day. One afternoon, I told that man about Jesusito, and Miguel described how he can only see shadows with his form of blindness, but that it is enough to help him distinguish the presence of vital objects such as doorways or vehicles. The more I saw, the more I was concerned about Jesús being able to function with his blindness as he grew older. Marysol and I went to work and looked into every facility or organization working with blind children. We quickly discovered there were very few specialized services or education for the blind in Cuenca. This especially hit home for us when we tried to start Jesús in kindergarten.

Marysol

Centro Educativo La Cometa was the name of the kindergarten Paz attended when she was three. She had done well there, and once we learned there was no preschool for blind or otherwise developmentally-disabled children in Cuenca, we approached the director at the school to see if Jesús could be enrolled there. Even though the school had never admitted a student with special needs, we were told Jesús could attend and were grateful and excited.

We hired a teacher to be with Jesús and help integrate him into the classes and activities—but after a couple of months, problems began. Some parents complained to the director, claiming Jesús was disruptive and wondering why a child like him was admitted in the first place. The teacher working with Jesús said there were often miscommunications between her and the director about how his learning challenges should be addressed. For his part, Jesús loved being at the school for the six months he attended. He was always a happy boy, thrilled to hear the voices of the other children and be part of a larger group.

Jesús was also more aware of the children around him. For example, the students and teachers celebrated each time a child completed potty training and no longer needed to wear a diaper. One evening, I tried to change Jesús into a fresh diaper and he pushed it away. He didn't want it, and after that he no longer needed one. As he learned control and self-motivation, he took care of another physical need

> I felt God was showing me His goodness and it eased my fears.

on his own. His doctors were indecisive about when to remove his cannula. Skin was starting to grow around it and we had to be careful with the area, placing tape over it, for example, when Jesús went swimming. In the pool one afternoon, Jesús not only removed the cannula by himself, but he controlled the opening and kept the skin closed watertight. He never used the cannula again. These self-directed behaviors encouraged me. I felt God was showing me His goodness and it eased my fears.

Ultimately, though, the school setting became too much for Jesús. It wasn't that the people at the school didn't want to help us.

They were simply ill-equipped to meet the social and educational demands Jesús presented. As the time for the next surgery on his face and nose approached, he took time off from school for the procedure and recovery. When it was time for him to return to the school, we decided to keep him home for good—and wondered what to do next.

Andrés regularly travelled to other cities in Ecuador and once each year to South America or Europe to attend sales conventions in support of his work at the jewelry store. He asked me to accompany him on a weeklong trip to Spain, and when we were there we were introduced to an organization called *ONCE*, the *Organization National Ciegos Espanoles*. Officials there took us to the *Museo Tiflologico* in Madrid, a unique museum ONCE created and maintains that is filled with models of buildings such as the Eiffel Tower made of iron, the Taj Mahal made of marble, and the ancient walls of the city of Jerusalem made of wood. Each *maqueta* is created for blind people to touch so they can learn about and "see" historical landmarks with their hands. Inspired by this, Andrés later approached a friend who was an architect and, in trade for a Swiss watch, the friend built a scale model of our home that Jesús could touch and take apart floor by floor.

Andrés

Upon our return from Spain, Marysol and I realized we needed to do more not just to help Jesús, but to benefit the entire blind population of Cuenca with their education and knowledge of the world around them. That's when we met Daniel Villavicencio, director of *Sociedad No Videntes del Azuay*, a private, non-profit organization helping the blind in Cuenca. As a teenager, Daniel Villavicencio was shot in the face with buckshot during a hunting trip, leaving him blind. Around the same time, we encountered three other individuals. One was Oswaldo Matute, a friend of Daniel's and a teacher of blind children. As an infant, Oswaldo was placed in an incubator with lights so bright they damaged his eyes, causing him to be blind. The other two were Ana Lucia Cabrera, a specialized teacher of the blind, and Dr. Santiago Jara, an attorney. After several meetings, Marysol and I joined with these four remarkable people to launch FAICE, the *Fundacion de Apoyo Integral al Ciego Ecuatoriano*, in May 2003. Written out in Braille, the letters of FAICE look like a bridge, and that's exactly what we were—a bridge of hope to connect those in need to those who want to fulfill that need.

No credible statistics existed about the blind population in the Province of Azuay or Cuenca, so Daniel spearheaded a field survey that was distributed in the mail through the city's water and electric bills and was also made available to parishioners in Catholic churches. Over fifty thousand surveys were distributed, allowing us to collect data on over six thousand people and families with some sort of blindness disability. We learned some incredible things. As it was with Oswaldo, medical malpractice was the cause of several of the cases of blindness. Some blindness was not total but caused either by low vision or having only one eye. A large proportion of the blind in Cuenca were children, and few blind people had enough education to be employable. Finally, many people did not possess canes, talking watches, Braille rulers, or other basic aids to help them cope with their condition.

Armed with these findings, FAICE went to work to address the needs. We organized an early intervention program. Blind children in Cuenca were entering the public school system by age seven, so our program targeted children from birth through age six. It provided a place for children and parents to receive one-on-one, customized speech and physical therapy, music therapy, and training in Braille, all at a minimal fee.

We had an average of fifteen families using the program at any given time. My role was to oversee fundraising for the foundation, particularly to raise money to buy devices such as gym equipment and canes. We also worked helping meet the needs of people with other disabilities because *Centro Cristiano de Cuenca* was able to import over one thousand wheelchairs and one million Mebandazole tablets to treat intestinal infections common in Ecuador. The wheelchairs came from Free Wheelchair Mission in California, and the medication from *Operacion Bendicion* through the 700 Club. We also contacted the CEDEI Foundation, which houses a bilingual university in Cuenca, to develop an international conference for teachers of the blind with the assistance of Valerie Moser, a special education teacher for the blind who would end up being a significant person in our lives, and especially for Jesús.

Just before we left for Florida to meet Valerie, our family was at *La Carolina* park in Quito when a little girl came up to Jesús, and just stared at him in awe. Then she turned and ran to her father, saying, "I want one for Christmas!" I realized she thought Jesús was a toy robot! She returned to Jesús and kept looking at him, fascinated. I took out my cellphone and pretended I was controlling "my robot" to support her assumption. The father of the little girl just turned red. Interestingly, some adults in Hispanic countries like Ecuador are ashamed to approach people with disabilities. Some blind people regularly stay indoors because they don't want to be outside where they'll

> We love when children and adults approach Jesús and ask us questions about him.

be stared at. But through Jesús, we've learned we need to be like little children—like the girl who thought he was a robot. She came with a pure heart; when she discovered he was a real boy, she was still happy to be near him. We love when children and adults approach Jesús and ask us questions about him.

The Florida trip was designed to help us learn more about organizations and services available in the United States to help the blind, and it coincided with two months of weekly treatments with an American ocularist on Jesús' tiny eye sockets. Jesús was now six years of age, and the two small prosthesis used on him during the treatments did not look like eyes but more like clear marbles, not perfectly round but oval to oblong depending on how the bones of his eye sockets needed to expand. We learned how to put them in and pop them out. At first, it took several of us to keep Jesús still while they were inserted, but he quickly adjusted and got used to them.

We learned a couple of things about the prosthesis marbles. First, they didn't float—discovered when one came out while in the swimming pool. We searched the bottom of the pool for an hour before a friend finally spotted it. Second, they bounce—which was most evident when we went to a cafeteria one morning for breakfast. Two elderly women were sitting at a table near us, and I noticed one of the ladies was staring in our direction, a look of utter confusion on her face. We kept eating, but a minute later I peered over again and saw she was struggling to eat. I started to get a little upset about it—until she suddenly screamed as if she'd seen a ghost. I looked at Jesús, saw his empty socket, and then looked down to see his tiny fake eye bouncing on the floor. Again, we laughed; what was a normal sight for us must've been downright frightening to others.

We first met Valerie at the Ft. Lauderdale Lighthouse for the

Blind after being introduced to that organization during an earlier visit to its sister facility in Miami. We had an appointment there for a tour from the director, and Valerie was working with children in a little gym when we first met her. She gestured for Jesús to come over to join her.

Marysol

Andrés and I loved the gentle, attentive way she interacted with Jesús. They played a bit and then she read a book to him, and she connected with him in a way no other teacher had in the past. She spoke with us, too, and it was then that we learned she was the early intervention teacher there and had been working with blind children for a quarter century. When the director expressed his eagerness for the Lighthouse to work with FAICE, I was so excited, and I knew we had to stay in contact with Valerie. After returning to Ecuador, we corresponded with her and developed a relationship that led to her coming to Cuenca for the seminar. There she showed our special education teachers, college-aged men and women, how to work with blind children. Valerie confidently and practically showed them how to guide a child, and her extraordinary hands-on training impacted me even more than her excellent lectures.

She had such energy for a woman in her sixties who was thriving despite her own low vision limitation because of a degenerative disease. As I watched her, I began to understand for the first time the difference between a child dealing with blindness alone versus a child like my Jesusito who was suffering with other disabilities in addition to blindness. As I perceived how underdeveloped Jesús was in comparison with the other children his age, my heart grew heavy. Gratefully, Valerie stayed at our home with us during the seminar, and together we reviewed books about how to raise a blind child. However, it was her ongoing example as she worked with Jesús that impacted me the most. "Remember, you need to describe to Jesús what is going on around him," she taught me. "He's not going to see you if you go across the room to the kitchen. Tell him, 'Jesús, I'm by your side. Now I'm going to get up and get a glass of water.'" Valerie's instruction empowered me to be a more effective mother to Jesús.

In the final days before she returned to the United States, Andrés and I told Valerie about our desire to someday live somewhere where Jesús would get the best possible education and services for the blindness and all of his other disabilities. "If Jesús was your son," Andrés asked, "where would you take him?" She mentioned two places in the western U.S.—Austin, Texas and Tucson, Arizona. The advice was appreciated, but it also raised a question for which we had no answer. *How were we going to get back to the United States to visit these cities, much less actually live in one of them?* We only possessed tourist visas that allowed us to stay in the U.S. for no more than six months at a time.

I faced this dilemma with more hope than before because of what God had done in our lives. At this time, Andrés and I started taking Bible Institute classes through our church. This further developed our knowledge of the Bible, as did the curriculums about Maximizing Manhood and Unique Womanhood that we were studying and teaching. I continued in this season of spiritual growth when internationally-renowned pastor Guillermo Maldonado of *El Rey Jesus* church in Miami, Florida and his team of assistant pastors visited our church in Cuenca. Maldonado was famous for his services where many creative miracles of the Lord occurred. We felt honored when our pastor Jimmy Cornejo asked us to join him and his wife in a private room behind the main platform to meet with Maldonado and his wife. Since Jesús was not with us that morning, Andrés pulled a photo of Jesús out of his Bible.

We talked, prayed, and showed him the photo of our son.

He looked at it. "Do you want to ask God for a miracle?" he asked.

I thought the question was strange. "Jesús is already a miracle," I countered. Andrés and I knew Jesús was already accomplishing so much more with his conditions than we or anyone else expected. We felt every one of those achievements were a miracle.

Maldonado held up the photo. "That's not the will of the Lord," he said in reference to Jesús' appearance. "Do you want a miracle, or do you not want a miracle?"

I suppose Maldonado was well-meaning, but his suggestion that Jesús was somehow not special, not precious—not whole—unless he was supernaturally healed of all of his disabilities offended my thinking. At the same time, though, a seed was planted in my heart that indeed God could fully heal Jesús physically, not because my son wasn't already a miracle, but to bring glory to Him. My trust in the Lord grew.

Two nights later, a group of Maldonado's assistant pastors visited our apartment. After a few moments of polite introduction, one of the pastors began crying.

"I have a passage for you from the Lord," he said, and he opened his Bible, a New King James Version, and began reading in Spanish. "Now as Jesus passed by, He saw a man who was blind from birth. And His disciples asked Him, saying, 'Rabbi, who sinned, this man or his parents, that he was born blind?' Jesus answered, 'Neither this man nor his parents sinned, but that the works of God should be revealed in him. I must work the works of Him who sent Me while it is day; the night is coming when no one can work. As long as I am in the world, I am the light of the world.' When He had said these things, He spat on the ground and made clay with the saliva; and He anointed the eyes of the blind man with the clay. And He said to him, 'Go, wash in the pool of Siloam' (which is translated, Sent). So he went and washed, and came back seeing."

As we listened, Andrés and I realized that it was from John chapter nine—the same passage we had chosen by chance from a CD cover for the invitation cards announcing the celebratory Mass in Cuenca to present Jesús to friends and family. More amazing, though, was the significance of what the story said to us as parents. We understood

> Jesús is here so that the works of God will be revealed in him.

that it was not because of the beggar's sin, or the sin of his parents, that he was blind. That realization brought healing to us, erasing the idea that Andrés and I may have somehow been responsible for Jesús' condition.

Even more, it spoke to us that Jesús is here so that the works of God will be revealed in him. Jesús—and everything that happened to him to the past and will happen to him in the future—was for God's glory!

Then came November 3, 2003 and my moment of divine confrontation. By then we had moved from our apartment to our home, a significant event not only because we were no longer renting but now paying a mortgage, but also because it provided much more space for Jesús and the girls to move about and gave each one of them rooms of their own. Jesús was getting up and down the stairs by himself, and he loved sitting on the indoor swing Andrés had installed on the third floor. Among our new neighbors was a woman who, like me, was from Mexico and had married an Ecuadorian man. One day her father, Pastor Paul Santana, visited her from Mexico and they invited our children and us on a picnic. Later, we returned to our home for dinner, and he asked a question I'd never been directly asked before: "When were you born again?"

Andrés shared about his experience in Guaymas. Then it was my turn to respond. I didn't understand then, as I do now, that I needed to be born again. I didn't know that we were born into Adam with a sinful nature that was disconnected from God, and therefore I needed to be born again as described by Jesus to Nicodemus in the third chapter of John. All I knew at that moment was that I needed to receive Christ, and I had already done that in my first communion.

"I know Christ. I love Him," I said. "He has been with me all of the time."

"Yes," he said with persistent gentleness. "But when did you give your life to Jesus Christ?"

I responded as I had before, not offended yet also not understanding exactly what he was asking. He discerned my confusion.

"Do you have the Life?" he asked. He opened his Bible and asked me to read 1 John 5:12: "He who has the Son has life; he who does not have the Son of God does not have life." He then asked again, "Do you have the Life?"

Suddenly I realized—I had knowledge of Jesús Christ and I believed in Him, but He had not been intentionally invited to dwell in me to have His Life, all of who He is and what He did, inside of me. It was like a sword passing through my heart and I started to cry. He then asked me, "Do you want to give your life completely to Jesus Christ this day and welcome Him to live inside of you?" Deeply moved, I responded, "Yes, this day, I give you everything, Lord, and I welcome Your life inside of me and I accept all that you have done for me."

My memory of that pivotal moment, and of how my faith in God had blossomed in my heart since then, infused me to trust Him more. My relationship with the Lord deepened even further when we were in Florida for Jesús' ocular treatments. We were in the Miami area, and I went online one Thursday to look up information about Ancient Paths seminars. First introduced to us by Eduardo and Ximena in Cuenca, that first experience was life-changing. Ancient Paths was offered by Family Foundations International (FFI). I discovered there was going to be an Ancient Paths' seminar that Saturday in Tampa, about a four-hour drive away from us. I contacted the email address given to see if there was a chance Andrés and I could still attend.

While I was in the kitchen doing the dishes, I prayed, "Lord, if it is your will for us to go, then you will show us." The very moment I concluded my prayer, Andrés said that Larry and Sue, the coordinators there, had just responded—and said we could come! I was thrilled, but we still had to find babysitting for the children in order for us to go. Thankfully, Andrés' cousins Leni and Ximena were living north of West Palm Beach and they agreed to watch the kids and meet Jesús' special care needs for the day. We went to their home Friday night and left the children with them when we departed the next morning at about 4:00 a.m.

Having never been to Tampa before, we had some trouble finding Larry and Sue's home and arrived a little late as a result. Nevertheless, they paused the seminar to welcome us into their home. There were eight other people there, and the meeting was being held in the living room. As we took our seats, I already sensed that God was doing something special in my life. On the drive from Miami to Tampa, we listened to an audio teaching about King David and how he danced and rejoiced without shame at the return of the Ark of the Covenant to Jerusalem. As I listened, I knew I wanted more of God and, like David, I didn't care what anyone thought about that. This desire for the Lord increased at the seminar as I watched the Ancient Paths video. I thought it was significant that I could perfectly understand the teachings in English even though, at that point, my understanding of the language wasn't as strong as it is today.

After the video, we broke up into small groups, and I couldn't wait to share what the Lord had been stirring up in my heart. I told the group about what God had done in my life up to that point and was surprised at my own vulnerability as I shared about an experience as a teenager when I lied. Only Andrés knew about this, and I felt that since then the incident had created a cycle of trying to cover myself through lying. When I was done, the facilitator asked, "When do you believe this tendency to not tell the truth started?" I didn't know—so I stopped myself and quietly asked the Lord to show me the answer right away. I'd never done anything like that before.

God didn't disappoint. The Lord Jesus helped me to remember an experience when I was only six years old where I believed that lying could protect me and others from problems because I was celebrated for not telling the truth.

I was amazed that God had showed me, in that moment, the answer. It was supernatural. Then the facilitator said, "Lord, you were there that moment with Marysol. What do you say?" I closed my eyes again. I was confused. *What can He possibly say?* I thought. Then I saw a light, bright and warm, and I felt a hand touch the side of my face and turn it toward the direction of the light. Then I heard a voice. It was God.

25

"You're precious," He said. It was as though He was saying to my spirit, 'Don't look at others. Don't look at yourself. Just look at me. You're precious.'" I thought of the Bible verse, "Looking unto Jesus the author and finisher of our faith; who for the joy that was set before him endured the cross, despising the shame, and is set down at the right hand of the throne of God." (Hebrews 12:2)

> I was amazed that God had showed me, in that moment, the answer.

I started crying and opened my eyes. "What happened?" asked the facilitator, and I shared with everyone what I had just experienced. Before then, I knew God was real, but this was the first time I felt He directly spoke to me in that way. Even more, the root of lying and the shame I felt from that root was gone. God had broken it! His truth was more powerful, and as John 8:32 says, "And you shall know the truth, and the truth shall make you free."

Andrés

That weekend was amazing, so when we learned later that Craig Hill, the leader of Family Foundations, was going to be a guest speaker at the *Salvamos a la Familia* seminar in Lima, Peru, we were thrilled when Pastor Jimmy Cornejo invited us to attend the event. After that conference we were blessed to be included in a trip to Cuzco and Machu Picchu to meet Craig and his wife Jan. On the journey in the train, I noticed that Craig looked like he wasn't feeling well. When I asked him about it, he said he had a fever and a headache. Knowing there wasn't a drug store available for miles, I reached in my backpack, opened a bottle, and tried to hand him some extra strength Tylenol. But instead of receiving the "thank you" I expected from my offer, he gave me a most unusual response.

"That's okay, Andrés," he said, his face pale and slick with sweat. "I don't like to put drugs in my body."

I was shocked. I thought, *Oh no! He is sicker than I thought. The fever must be affecting his brain.* I couldn't understand how he could reject the only medicine available to him in such a remote place.

He went on to share how he was already fighting the bacteria attacking his immune system. He told me about a company that uses glyconutrients, blends of plant-sourced saccharides, and other natural remedies instead of pharmaceuticals. With my degree in biochemistry engineering, I was intrigued to learn more and was compelled to tell him about Jesús' persistent illnesses, as well as the advice we had received from Valerie about the two places in the United States where Jesús may be able to receive the medical help, education, and services he needed.

"We're going to have a *Manna Relief* conference in Dallas," Craig said. "Why don't you and Marysol come to Texas with your children? You'd learn more about this non-profit organization and how its glyconutrients can help Jesús and your family. You could even drive down to Austin to see if you like it there."

Feeling that God was orchestrating this opportunity, we accepted Craig's offer and attended the conference in Texas. At that time, we had no idea the positive impact these glyconutrients were going to have on the life of our Jesús, the children of FAICE, and our entire family. Upon visiting Austin, we went to visit the state's school for the deaf and blind there, and they told us we needed to be residents to be accepted into the school—and the same limitation applied to the state school for the deaf and blind in Tucson. We also decided we didn't like the city of Austin; it was larger than we expected and simply wasn't someplace we wanted to live. We returned to Dallas for the rest of the *Manna*

Relief conference knowing Austin was out of the picture. We believed God was going to give us a solution.

It didn't take Him long. Knowing our need, Craig proposed that he become a sponsor for the religious worker visas required for us to actually live in the United States—and that we join Family Foundations and move to Tucson. In college I had visited Tucson and assured Marysol that we would enjoy living there because it was a family-friendly city. Compelled by Jesús' need and God's prompting, I resigned from my position at my grandfather's jewelry store and turned over the directorship of FAICE to Paul Moreno and his wife Lorena, who kindly offered to help us through their generosity and sacrifice so that we could make the move. We rented out our home, sold most of our possessions, and filled no less than twenty-two suitcases to take with us. We were willing to leave all of the comforts we had in Ecuador, as well as our collective comfort zone, to go to the United States.

In November 2007, we arrived in Albuquerque, New Mexico and were then transported to a church retreat center in the nearby mountains in Glorieta to join other Family Foundations members from all over the world attending the annual international FFI conference with speakers invited by Craig Hill such as Robert Sterns and Sid Roth. Through their presentation, we learned for the first time about the Hebraic roots of Christianity, causing a paradigm shift in our theology. In addition, Craig asked for people to come forward to the platform if they had any prayer needs. We went up with only Jesús at our side since the girls were at a kid's camp elsewhere on the property. Craig introduced us to the crowd and everyone prayed for us. Some came forward and laid hands on us; others stayed and prayed from their seats.

> We believed God was going to give us a solution.

It was a thrill to feel so loved and included and experience the unity of God's people. Of course, we had no idea then that an entire team of people had been praying in Tucson for God to send them a couple who could serve as Spanish liaisons, nor did we know that one of the nation's largest Family Foundations teams, led by Jim and Linda Floyd, who became our mentors and very dear to us, were located in Tucson. We also didn't know how we were going to get our voluminous luggage there, or even where we were going to live permanently once we arrived.

We were now in the United States—and were anxious to see what God was going to do next.

Chapter 7

"It's coming..."

Marysol

The Family Foundations gathering at Glorieta was inspiring. Yet I couldn't help but feel anxious about all of the unknowns ahead for our family, especially for the children. The Lord soothed my mother's heart, though, as He began to immediately take care of those needs.

First, a couple named Dennis and Judy welcomed us to stay in their home in central Tucson until we could find a place of our own. They were longtime friends of Felipe Calderon, the very person Andrés visited Tucson with as a student twenty-five years earlier. Next, several Family Foundations members who lived in Tucson volunteered to help transport every piece of our luggage in their vehicles. Car after car was loaded up and led the way on the day-long drive from Glorieta to Tucson while we followed along in our rental car, Andrés and I riding up front while the three kids sat in the back seat. The modern-day wagon train arrived in Tucson just prior to Thanksgiving. We spent our first Thanksgiving in the United States as guests in the home of Jim and Linda Floyd. We enjoyed their food and fellowship and it was important for us to be able to celebrate the holiday and be thankful for everything God had already done for us in just our first few days in the United States. We felt welcomed as though we were part of their family, and we felt so overwhelmed by the generosity toward us from all the FFI team.

Finally, Dennis and Judy's home was located next door to Robinson Elementary School, where we knew Jesús, Paz, and Sofi would start attending school after the Christmas holiday. We then learned that Robinson just happened to have a good special education program and was the top referral school to the Arizona School for the Deaf and Blind (ASDB) located on the west side of the city.

Many could claim all of these events as being mere coincidences, but I didn't believe that. Andrés and I started calling them "God-incidences" and looked ahead in expectation of what He was going to do next. Since the kids were already enrolled at Robinson, Andrés focused his attention on finding us a house and a vehicle. We didn't know then how long we'd need to live with Dennis and Judy, but we wanted to find our own place as soon as we could. We had two rooms in their home; one was for Andrés and me and the three kids shared the other. It was crowded and chaotic, but we were so grateful. When the children started school right after Thanksgiving weekend, it was a new and difficult experience for them and for me as a mother. I remember the coldness of the season and how it mirrored the uncertainty in my soul as I wondered what was coming next for my children. Jesús in particular was not accustomed to getting up and out early in the morning for a daylong schedule. In addition, Jesús was placed in the classroom based on his age. By then he was seven years old and was therefore put into a first grade class, though in reality he was still at a preschool level academically.

He was also in a class with other children with various developmental disabilities; each one different but none with his unique condition. Sofi was placed in kindergarten and Paz in third grade. Each girl spoke very little English, so they picked up the language at school, in conversation with Dennis and Judy, and by watching educational television on Public Broadcasting Service.

For all of us, the adjustment to school was challenging. Paz did not complain, but we could see how she was struggling to make new friends and understand the different subjects. Sometimes Andrés or I went in to sit with Sofi so that she wouldn't feel afraid; other times he or I joined Jesús in his classroom to help him feel more comfortable. Usually happy and bright, Jesús was often edgy and crying when he got home. He beat himself on his head to indicate that he was frustrated. It was nothing more than a transition, but it was still hard.

During all of this time, Jesús' two classroom teachers and a team of specialists, each of whom worked with the developmentally disabled children for forty-five minutes each week, were assessing Jesús to determine if he should be transferred to ASDB. Andrés and I asked God for our Jesús to be able to attend this highly sophisticated school for the blind, which in our minds was the major reason for our immigration.

Andrés

Marysol and I weren't sure what to expect when we walked up to Robinson the morning of Jesús' Individualized Education Program (IEP) evaluation. We were there to meet with the pair of teachers and team of specialists who had evaluated our son over the past several weeks in speech, mobility, and a variety of other developmental areas. We were ushered into a meeting room and took our seats at an oval table with the other teachers. They knew Jesús' medical history and were aware that he had already been through six major surgeries. Each one spoke of the positive impact Jesús had made on them through his kindness and gentle spirit, and then reported on what they had observed and shared their recommendations. Their conclusion: Jesús was ready to go to the Arizona School for the Deaf and Blind. We were pleased, excited, and grateful.

"Thank you," I said. "My wife and I always like to thank God for what He is doing in the life of our son, and we would like to pray."

Prayer is allowed at a school during school hours, but a teacher cannot recommend or lead it. My request, however, was welcomed. "Yes," one of the teachers said. "Please do."

> They were inspired by our son's smile, joy, and presence.

Lord, I want to honor you and thank you for each one of the people here in this room. Thank you for the opportunity to have this kind of school available to us, and for these teachers who have been so concerned about our son. Lead Jesús' life in every way at the new school. To you be the glory and honor. In the name of Jesus Christ we pray, Amen.

It was a simple prayer of thankfulness, but I could tell it was appreciated by the teachers. To this day, Marysol and I believe that they were open to allowing our prayer that day because of how they were inspired by our son's smile, joy, and presence. God clearly had the last word at that meeting. We saw it as yet another miracle of how God was using our son and family to touch the lives of others.

Marysol

God loves each one of the many professionals that He has brought into our lives to work with Jesús. They have such a heart for Jesús and other children like him with special needs. As a mother, I appreciate them and their dedication and sacrifice—and with the approval of the transfer, I looked forward to meeting more caring professionals at ASDB. First, though, I was just as excited about moving into the house Andrés had found for us.

It was located just a few blocks north of Dennis and Judy's home. That was important to me because I felt like our family was secure in that neighborhood. At one thousand square feet, it was still far smaller than our home in Ecuador, but after living in two rooms for the previous two months, its small kitchen, dining room, and living room were positively spacious in comparison, as were the three bedrooms and one bathroom. Because I always had helpers in my home in Ecuador to manage daily chores while I cared for Jesús and the girls and met my responsibilities at FAICE, I now had to get used to taking care of all of the cooking, cleaning, and other household chores on my own. Certainly, Andrés helped with those chores and I enjoyed my expanded homemaker roles, but it was at times overwhelming— so much so that I became ill, for the first time in years, shortly after we moved into the larger home.

During that illness, though, God did something remarkable. I woke up in the middle of the night to go to the restroom. As I walked down the hall, I heard God's voice in my mind. He said, "I am going to teach you to be a daughter, and you are going to see me as your Daddy." Just as He had months earlier in Glorieta, the Lord lovingly soothed my heart, assuring me that He was going to help me to learn to trust Him and, even more importantly, rest in Him. All of my life, even before the birth of Jesús, I struggled with the stress of my responsibilities and questioned my abilities as a wife and mother. Now God was using this new situation in a new country to bring further healing to my fears and doubts.

Andrés

As I assisted Marysol at home, I was also overseeing our work as Hispanic liaison facilitators for Family Foundations. Tucson's Harvest Media Ministries trained me and provided the recording studios so that I could voice the Spanish-language narratives for Craig Hill's video seminars. Marysol and I also served as co-facilitators of Family Foundations' events at churches in Tucson, and Jim and Linda, the couple that hosted us at Thanksgiving and became our Mentor Coordinators to help us advance from being facilitators to coordinators for the ministry, trained us. It was a rewarding but busy time for both of us, and it was not unusual for the children to go with us on weekends to the churches, occupying themselves in classrooms under the watch of volunteers while we worked at the events. Still, we found our moments to go out together as a family. One night at Chick-Fil-A, we were eating when a big, tall man walked up to our table. He was Hispanic and, I guessed, Mexican.

Do I know you?" he asked. He had a strange expression; goofy and a bit disconcerting. "No," I responded.

"Are you Christians?" he asked, his features softening just a bit. "Yes, we are."

He smiled and was joined by a woman. He introduced them as Manlio and Dalila, and I asked them to join us. It turned out they were more than friendly and became the first Hispanic couple we knew in Tucson. "Would you like to come to our church for a visit?" he asked before the meal was over. "It's called *Centro Cristiano Carismatico*." The name was practically identical to our church in Ecuador, and we dropped in the following Sunday. We were glad we did. I was especially overwhelmed by the worship experience. It was intense and anointed, and Marysol and I immediately felt we were home.

A few weeks later we were at the close of the service. The children had just rejoined us in the sanctuary after returning from their children's services elsewhere on the campus. We were lingering as we usually did, some people filing out and others still worshipping, when Héctor came up to me. I'd never formally met Héctor but knew him to be a person believed by the pastor and congregation to possess the gift of prophecy. Like Manlio, Hector had an unusual expression on his face. It was pensive and serious. He spoke in Spanish—and said two words.

Ya viene. It's coming.

"Yes," I replied. "Jesus is coming."

"I'm not talking about that," he said. "Jesus is coming, I know. But his miracle is coming." He pointed at Jesús. "I've been watching you. God is going to perform a creative miracle in the life of your son."

I was speechless, but in my mind I was screaming. *Is this from God?*

Hector assured me that he was not a false prophet, and that he tells the pastor the things that he declares to others, and that many of his words have come to pass. Of course, I wanted to believe him. I could tell by the expression on Marysol's face that she did as well. After all, this was the first time anyone had specifically used the words "creative miracle" in reference to Jesús. It was exciting—and frightening.

"Thank you, Hector," I finally uttered. "We believe." And my audible words echoed the unspoken longing of my heart.

Marysol

Hector's prophecy was another instance where I felt like God was drawing me to the idea that my life—my entire family's life—was going to have a purpose greater than the day-to-day existence I'd been living for so long, and especially since our move to the United States. I felt as though I was doing nothing more than surviving, handling my vital responsibilities as a wife, a mother, and in ministry with Family Foundations, but nothing more. My spirit was yearning for a deeper sense of significance and impact, and as I prayed and reflected on this longing, God gave me thoughts and verses that I habitually jotted down on envelopes or pieces of paper and often left scattered here and there throughout the house. It was my way of chronicling what I believed God was saying to me, even if I couldn't quite put it all together as of yet.

> My spirit was yearning for a deeper sense of significance and impact.

A repeated area of Scripture in my musings was selections from the book of Isaiah. There was Isaiah 43:1-3, which I felt God gave me for Jesús during his second surgery. "Fear not, for I have redeemed you; I have called you by your name; You are Mine. When you pass through the waters, I will be with you; And through the rivers, they shall not overflow you. When you walk through the fire, you shall not be burned, Nor shall the flame scorch you. For I am the Lord your God, The Holy One of Israel, your Savior." Before that Scripture came to me, there was Isaiah 61:1-3, which we handed to Andrés and me during a verse exchange ceremony at a New Year's Eve service. As I read it, it called to mind a vision I had six months earlier in which I saw my family taking people out of a dark pit and into a magnificent light. "He has sent Me to heal the brokenhearted, To proclaim liberty to the captives, And the opening of the prison to those who are bound; To proclaim the acceptable year of the Lord, And the day of vengeance of our God; To comfort all who mourn,

To console those who mourn in Zion, To give them beauty for ashes, The oil of joy for mourning."

Whenever the Lord gave me a word of encouragement or a passage from the Bible, I wrote it down, believing that somehow He would use my written remembrances for His purposes.

Andrés

We were especially tired one Saturday night at the conclusion of a three-day Ancient Paths seminar. It was special because Shawn and Martha, coordinators we had first met years earlier at our very first Ancient Paths seminar in Cuenca, had travelled from California to Tucson to serve with us as co-facilitators at this conference. The ministry to us and through us to all the participants and to all of us on the FFI team was rich and encouraging. So, it was with a sense of fulfillment and rest that I went to sleep that night—and had a dream that changed my life.

It was brief and profound. It didn't take place at any particular location or at any discernible time. I recall nothing being in a background of what I saw. All I remember was that I saw our Jesucito, just his face, looking away but then turning toward me. He was smiling. He had eyes, full and colored a light sky blue, gleaming and bright. It was as though I could reach out and touch him, cradle his face in my hands, pull him close to my chest—

I woke up, fully awake, and saw early morning sunlight casting its glow on the bedroom window. Then the tears came, stinging my eyes. I got up and made my way to the living room. I was heading toward my office to get my Bible. As I walked I prayed silently from the very depths of my soul, *Lord, if this dream is from you, you need to confirm it with Scripture.*

As a passed the kitchen, I saw a paper, folded up like a napkin, sitting near the stove. Through my sobs, I wiped my eyes to read what it said. It was in Marysol's handwriting.

> Isaiah 42:6-7 (NIV). I, the Lord, have called you in righteousness; I will take hold of your hand. I will keep you and will make you to be a covenant for the people and a light for the Gentiles, to open eyes that are blind, to free captives from prison, and to release from the dungeon those who sit in darkness.

I had little reaction to the first verse, but when I read, "To open blind eyes," I started to cry like a baby. *Yes. Yes, Lord!* I went to get my Spanish Bible and opened it to Isaiah 42 so that I could find the passage Marysol had written down. Then I read verses eight and nine and felt a wave of joy gush through me.

> "I am the Lord, that is My name; And My glory I will not give to another, Nor My praise to carved images. Behold, the former things have come to pass, And new things I declare; Before they spring forth I tell you of them." (Isaiah 42:8-9)

I wept again, and then hurried to the bedroom to wake up Marysol. I told her about the dream, about finding the verse she had written down, about reading the rest of the passage in my Bible—everything! *This is it!* I thought as Marysol tried to process what I had just shared.

> Jesús was going to be healed so God, and Him alone, would get the glory!

This is the harbinger! The harbinger of the miracle He was going to do for His glory but using the life of our son Jesús!

I knew God was going to be powerfully revealed when it happened. Jesús' life was not just so a saint could get her due, like had been suggested. It wasn't so Andrés and Marysol could get any credit for being wonderful parents. It wasn't even so Paz and Sofi could be hailed as the caring sisters they were.

No. Jesús was going to be healed so God, and Him alone, would get the glory!

Ya viene.

It's coming indeed!

Marysol

By now, Jesús had been at the Arizona School for the Deaf and Blind for a while and was getting used to being on a regular schedule. The biggest breakthrough was that he was able to ride the school bus on his own to and from the ASDB campus across town. It was exciting and a bit frightening to watch him transition from being more like a baby boy, like he was in Cuenca, to now being more like a child his age. It wasn't easy for him. In the past, he hardly complained or cried, even when he was ill or after his surgeries. He was like a little angel. But now he was moody and got upset more often. Jesús observed how the other kids at school acted out to get attention and started emulating their behavior. He even began scratching us when he was especially angry.

Paz and Sofi didn't like it, either; besides, they were going through their own transitions as they adjusted to a new school, Calvary Chapel Christian School, and the rigors of making new friends and fitting in. Andrés sensed my stress and knew that the home we were in near Dennis and Judy's home, while a blessing, was still a bit small for our family. Eventually, he found a home that we could rent that was larger, more modern, and located just a few blocks away from the girls' school. It was a positive change for all of us.

Andrés

In late October 2010, Marysol and I were asked to travel to Houston, Texas to help facilitate an Ancient Paths seminar and establish a culture of blessing at Grace Community, the second-largest Hispanic church in that huge city. Pastor David Scarpeta and his wife Diana invited us there. David's mother-in-law had suggested they have an Ancient Paths seminar at their church after her experience of having been wonderfully ministered to by Ancient Paths in her homeland of Bogotá, Colombia.

Just over sixty people attended our "Empowering Relationships" Ancient Paths seminar, and right after the conclusion of the service on Sunday, October 24, Pastor Alan, one of the pastors in the group I facilitated, asked to speak to Marysol and me alone. Jesús and the girls were still away enjoying the children's ministries at the church. We found a quiet place apart from the crowd.

"God has shown me that the miracle for your son is coming," he said. "It will be a creative miracle, and I feel God wants me to tell you that it can happen at any time. It can happen even while he is sleeping. Be aware that you could go into his room one morning, and the miracle will be there."

This was something new that had not been said by anyone else before—and it birthed more expectation in my heart. I always thought Jesús' miracle was going to happen in a church service or at a revival meeting with a minister. But the idea that it could happen in the privacy of our own home? *What are we* going to do if we go in to wake him up one morning and he has new eyes and a new nose? Will Jesús be scared? Will he be happy? It was thrilling—and also a bit frightening.

Marysol

When Pastor Alan shared his word from the Lord with us, it also created hope within me similar to Andrés. But more than that, I heard God speaking to my spirit, "Marysol my daughter, I've urged you to wake up and believe in what I have in store. Now I want you to expand your possibilities. You've placed Me in a box, thinking I will do my will in a certain way. But I can do anything! Let Me be who I am as God!" Again, the Lord was challenging me to go to a deeper place of trust in Him. Andrés always envisioned Jesús being healed in a service featuring a well-known pastor or healer, with lots of people gathered around and praying for our son. But I thought if his healing comes in the way Pastor Alan said it could, there's no way a specific person or particular event could take the glory for it. God, and only God, will get the glory! And He says in Isaiah 42:8, "My glory I will not give to another."

> Again, the Lord was challenging me to go to a deeper place of trust in Him.

This new expectation continued to resonate in my heart as we returned home and planned for the start of the New Year. As we entered into 2011, Jesús continued his classes at ASDB and the girls were doing well at Calvary, where they were getting a strong educational and spiritual foundation and earning various academic awards in writing, reading, and mathematics. By that summer, though, we learned that we had to leave the rental home because it had been sold, so we placed everything into storage before leaving for a combination vacation / ministry seminar trip to California. We were joined by my mother-in-law from Ecuador who was visiting us for the summer. By the time we got back, we didn't have a place to live and spent a few nights in a hotel and even stayed a few days on the Harvest Media Ministries property. It was chaotic and none of us slept well, especially Jesús. Eventually, we were able to find another home to rent and settled in as best we could.

The kids started another semester of school that fall, and we began to look forward to our first Covenant Marriage Weekend presented by Family Foundations—a time that was going to bring our most vivid harbinger yet.

Chapter 8

"Just dare to believe!"

Andrés

The three-day event was in October at Emmanuel Fellowship in Cottonwood, Arizona, a small community close to the picturesque red rock vistas of Sedona. At the end of the second day of the retreat, we sat outside at our hotel, took in the cool air, and completed our homework for review the following morning. We went up to our room and went soundly asleep—until my dream brought a glorious interruption to our slumber.

This time, I not only saw Jesús with eyes, but he also had a nose, pink and perfectly formed as well rosy cheeks. My son's face was up close, filled with joy, and he spoke to me, over and over.

"Hola Papá! Hola Papá!"

I responded, "Hola Mijo! Hola Mijo!"

Also, unlike my previous dream, there was a backdrop, fuzzy but discernible, of a stage and a person on the platform whose name, my mind told me, was Troy. Whatever he was, a pastor or prophet or healer, he had apparently just prayed for Jesús before my son turned to me and talked.

I woke up weeping, and immediately shook Marysol's shoulders. She eased herself awake.

Marysol

Andrés often wakes me up in the middle of the night, usually to pray about something burdening his heart, so the fact that he woke me up was not a surprise. What was unusual was that he was both crying and laughing at the same time. As soon as he recognized I was aware and ready to listen, he told me everything he saw in his dream—and, shockingly, I suddenly remembered the dream I had that same night sometime while I was asleep.

Oh, God, I thought. *You are talking to us.*

In my dream, I was with Jesús, though I don't know where or when. His face appeared as it is now, but then out of nowhere two round, clear circles appeared over his eye sockets, and the inside of these circles started churning, slowly at first but then faster, like two whirlpools of water. They spun and spun and then *pop!* His eyes appeared! It was as though God was allowing me to actually *see* the creative miracle take place!

> *Oh, God,* I thought. *You are talking to us.*

When I shared this with Andrés after he had told me about his dream, we knew—we just knew—that God was telling us that Jesús was going to be healed. We lay there and cried, worshipping the Lord and sensing His holy presence.

Both of us had dreamed about our son's creative miracle on the same night!

Andrés

Shortly after we started attending *Casa de Adoración*, a daughter church *of Centro Cristiano Carismatico* that was close to our home, a young woman named Patricia, known in the congregation as a person who receives words of knowledge from the Lord, approached us after the service. Marysol and I had just joined many others that morning in answering an altar call from Pastor Francisco Dominguez to come forward for prayer. Jesús was with us, and the pastor prayed for us and for him. I watched as Patricia spoke to the pastor and received his permission to share her word with us, and then she approached.

"I just want to let you know," she said, "that you are in the right place. The Lord has told me that what you have been asking for, you will see with your own eyes."

It was encouraging—especially since we were new at the church. A few weeks later, Pastor Dominguez confirmed the same message as he spoke from the pulpit. There was no doubt. God was continuing to inspire our faith, broaden our trust in Him, and prepare our hearts for all that He was communicating to us through our dreams and His people.

Marysol

A few months later saw the advent of 2012 and my decision to attend a special service at Victory Worship Center featuring a guest speaker named Dutch Sheets. I knew nothing about him, his ministry, or his book called *Intercessory Prayer*. He told some amazing stories from his book to inspire us to have the courage to pray for the impossible. In one, Sheets had traveled to a remote village in Guatemala to assist in building shelters for those whose homes had been destroyed by an earthquake. Each evening of their visit, he and the team held a service and preached the Gospel. He was about to preach on the final night of their stay when a team member told him about a little girl they had discovered on the far side of the village. She was tied to a tree. The girl was no more than seven years of age. Her parents explained that she was crazy, uncontrollable, and tried to hurt herself and others when they tried to untie her. They felt they had no other choice but to keep the girl bound.

Sheets was heartbroken and heard the Lord direct him on what to say to the villagers. "Tell them you are going to pray for the insane little girl … in the name of this Jesus you've been preaching about. Tell them that through Him you are going to break the evil powers controlling her—that when she is free and normal, they can then know that what you are preaching is true." Placing faith over his fear, Sheets prayed as God directed. The girl was set free from evil and the villagers accepted Christ as Lord! God wanted to do a miracle and used Sheets was the distributor of that miracle.

> God can do the impossible for His glory and purposes.

For most of my life, I had a mentality about prayer to not be selfish but humbly satisfied with all that God has done for me. Even after the birth of Jesús and the start of the harbingers, I still felt satisfied that God had done enough for us; that it was almost arrogant to expect more, much less ask for it. But that mindset was changed after first seeing and hearing other believers' testimonies, and pastors declare how God can do the impossible for His glory and purposes, and then finally hearing Dutch Sheets. During his presentation, he said that in each generation, the Lord has set aside people to be used of Him to distribute miracles as ambassadors of His love and salvation. He also said that each generation has those set apart to be recipients of miracles—and I accepted that message for my family and me. He closed in prayer and released a mantle of faith upon any in the congregation who wanted it. I received it that morning and felt my trust and reliance on God increase.

My experience at the service that day changed how I pray. I used to pray regarding Jesús' healing, "Lord, if it is your will, okay; but if it is not your will, that's okay with me, too." Now I realize that it is appropriate to boldly pray in confidence and embrace what Jesus did on the cross for us, knowing that God loves us and is a God of miracles who wants to do miracles. Jesus Christ didn't come to Earth and say to people, "Be sick—be sick." He declared "Be healed!" God desires us to be brought to a place where we realize that He is able to perform the impossible, but it is in His perfect timing, while in the meanwhile He reveals our identity in Him and more of Himself to us. And just like Daniel in the Bible, who prayed earnestly and waited for an answer only to learn from an angel of God that the answer had been delayed for twenty-one days because of a war in the heavenlies, we know there is often a spiritual battle that precedes the miracle. Through it all, God was continuing to help me understand Him better as my Father and to build my faith in Him as His daughter.

As the year progressed, Jesús continued his development at ASDB and the girls moved forward in their education at Calvary, but Jesús' needs were proving to be an increasing challenge when we attended church. Even before our time at *Casa de Adoración*, I had to come to terms with the fact that churches are ill-equipped to handle Jesús in their child care or other children's ministries. The people at every church are well-meaning, of course; it's just that the majority of the churches aren't able to provide proper care and attention for special needs children. Our typical experience started with Jesús acting out, crying or otherwise being disruptive to the point that I, and sometimes Andrés, had to get him and stay with him in the church foyer, or sometime even outside, until the service was over. At *Casa de Adoración*, his behavior improved for a while because the congregation was smaller, but even there his difficulties eventually returned. This ongoing circumstance, combined with the amount of traveling required for our Family Foundations' responsibilities, left me frustrated and tired. Still, God provided perspective and strength as we move onward into another year.

Andrés

By now it was 2013 and Jesús was twelve years of age. One of the results of his disabilities is that he is about the size of a seven-year-old child. One Sunday morning after church, Marysol and I were walking to our car in the *Casa de Adoración* parking lot when we noticed Patricia Pesqueira pulling her car into a space near us. She was apparently getting ready to drive home when she felt compelled to stop and talk to us. All of us at *Casa de Adoración* understood that Patricia received visions from God. She pulled down her car window.

"I have something to tell you," she said. "I had a vision of your son. He was grown up. His bones were stretched like a child of his age."

I marveled in my heart, *It's too much to ask for.* She didn't see Jesús' eyes or his nose like the others. This was an entirely different creative miracle, one that in combination with the others would essentially make our son completely whole. *But with God, there is no such thing as asking for too much,* I thought. Marysol and I looked at each other with fresh tears of joy.

> God kept giving us one harbinger of a miracle after another.

From South America to the United States, from Houston to Tucson, from one church to another, and from our bed in a hotel in Cottonwood to the one in our own home, God kept giving us one harbinger of a miracle after another. Over the years it had been different places, different people, different methods—each with a message that built upon the next one, revealing more of His big picture, birthing greater faith and hope. Often, I wonder, *What more can we do to make this happen, Lord?* Each time He responds, "You don't have to do anything. I am God. I am at work in your lives, and that is what it matters. Let me be me. It will happen. Just dare to believe!"

The Lord's faithful encouragement has been vital—especially since the entire time we've lived in the United States, our ability to stay in the country has been dependent on our religious worker visas being renewed every year-and-a-half. It was a constant struggle, requiring repeated letters from Craig Hill to the Department of Homeland Security that argued why we were of value to the country. We had been trained in various biblical studies of the Assemblies of God and other Christian ministries, but because we were not serving here as pastors of a church, U.S. immigration officials consistently questioned our need to stay in the country. Although our visas were always renewed, there was another obstacle to overcome. The income to pay for our living expenses came from donations sent from our family in Ecuador. Because immigration officials did not see these funds as "wages," we could never apply for residency in the United States. That changed in 2012 when we arranged for the donations to go to Family Foundations first so that it could then pay us what was considered to be wages. After two years of receiving those wages, we were allowed to apply for full residency.

When we first applied in 2014, we were initially turned away because our application apparently was not complete. With the assistance of Claudia, our immigration attorney, we corrected those perceived issues and prepared to reapply. Our interview with immigration was set for September 3, 2014. Claudia advised us that because religious visas were, in her words, "light" visas, applications for residency from people holding religious visas were easily denied. She added, "And I hope that you don't get one of the two new immigration officials that moved here from Phoenix. She is very strict." Understanding her metaphor, we rooted to get the other person—but, sure enough, our meeting was with the tougher individual. Yet Marysol and I did not lose hope; we had already decided that God was in control. If we became U.S. residents, it was great; but if we had to return to Ecuador or live in Mexico, we were ready for that, too.

Paz, Sofi, and Jesús waited out in the lobby as we went into the meeting room. Claudia took a seat in the back of the room, and Marysol and I went forward to meet the official. Before taking my seat, I placed the massive stack of papers—all the information imaginable on our family, as well as our justification to become residents—on the table. I figured we were going to need it.

As the official began her questioning, we noticed no change to her stern demeanor. Her posture was rigid, and her face was sour, but I couldn't help but notice that her necklace had a shiny Star of David pendant. By then we had been attending Congregation Beth Sar Shalom, a Messianic Jewish synagogue, for over a year on Saturdays while attending our Hispanic church on Sunday. *Okay*, I thought, *she may not be Messianic, but she is a Jew. That's good, because our Lord is a Jew.*

"What church do you go to?" she asked.

I listed the churches we'd attended in the past since arriving in Tucson, and she remained unmoved. Then I got to Congregation Beth Sar Shalom.

Her voice rose an octave and, for the first time, I heard what sounded like joy. "Beth Sar Shalom," she said. "That's *my* church!"

From that moment onward, there was an immediate connection between the official and me. We talked for what had to have been an hour about *Yeshua* and my research on what I have discovered to be a cross over Tucson based on outlining certain geographic points of historical significance dating back three centuries from the city's Christian history. She went to her computer and showed me a mountain summit in Israel that has the shape of the Hebrew letters for the word Jehovah. We gabbed and laughed. It was remarkable! I looked back at Claudia and her expression of shock was priceless. She couldn't believe what she was seeing. The official and I kept talking, and after a while Claudia excused herself, she said, for another appointment. Upon her departure, the official became even friendlier. She even invited the children into the meeting room so that she could meet them.

After answering a few more questions, the official stood up. "Wait here; maybe we have some visas." I wasn't sure what she meant by that, but moments later she returned. "Guess what?" she said. "Normally this is not the process and it takes weeks, but because of my position, I can do this. Congratulations. You are now U.S. residents." She came around the table and hugged us, and even posed for pictures with us.

> "Congratulations. You are now U.S. residents."

Marysol

When she said those words, I thought back to what I was thinking when we first arrived at her office. I saw on her wall a picture of the Twin Towers in New York City on fire after the terrorist attacks of September 11, 2001 and discerned from it that she cared about the country. When she started questioning us, I also felt compassion for her. Then, when she and Andrés started talking about Jesus (Yeshua), the cross over Tucson, and everything else, I sat quietly (not that I could get a word in edgewise) and admired my husband. Andrés is plain and straightforward, outgoing and bold no matter whom it is that he is speaking to. It is a gift that the Lord has given him. I was amazed at the conversation between the two of them and was happy and grateful that God gifted me with Andrés.

Most of all, her response and our residency confirmed it: God's will was for us to stay in the United States. We planned then to apply for U.S. citizenship when it is first available to us in 2019.

In the meantime, our family has continued to navigate new changes. Jesús' time at ASDB ended in December 2013, and after finishing his education through eighth grade at public schools, we awaited the next breakthrough for his educational needs. It came with his attendance at Cienega High School after our move to our new home in the Vail School District at the end of 2015. We discovered it was the best district for special needs students in the Tucson area, and Jesús has thrived there. All of the teachers have been wonderful with Jesús, and he has responded well both academically at the school, and through the respite and rehabilitation care provided for us at our home through Linda Patten, who has become a wonderful friend to Jesucito and to all our family.

Because of her academic excellence, Paz was granted a scholarship to attend Grand Canyon University in Phoenix. Sofi is attending Empire High School in Tucson. Led by God, we also left *Casa de Adoración* to begin attending Passion Church in February 2015 with Pastor Bob and Carolyn Sawvelle. Pastor Bob is author of the book *Receive Your Miracle Now: A Case for Healing Today.* Passion Church is known for being a ministry where miracles happen, and the presence of God is passionately sought. The love, encouragement, and ministry we are receiving there, combined with the continued evolution of our work with Family Foundations, led us to move forward with the writing of this book and to promote the book and its message—while furthering our desire to bring God's hope and faith to families, keep growing in our intimacy with the Lord, and promote and seek revival and unity in the Christian community in Tucson.

Our residency status has had an immediate and wonderful impact on Jesús. While no one else in our family can be eligible to receive full health benefits from the government until we someday become citizens, Jesús can receive benefits as though he were already a U.S. citizen because of his disabled status. In the eighteen months since that remarkable day in the immigration official's office, Jesús started language therapy, gymnastics, and music and horse therapy. It's been such a joy as a mother to see Jesús respond to the exhortations of Libby, the gymnastic teacher, to not give up when he cries and claims he can't complete an exercise. He's learning to do so much more on his own and though his own initiative. He is becoming more independent and confident with each passing day, a unique, one-in-a-million four-leaf clover through whom God shines forth.

We've also taken Jesús to various doctors and specialists in hopes of receiving new insights on his conditions and what could be done to help him. Time after time, the tests and procedures have been conducted and the answer has been the same—Jesús is a healthy, happy boy, but there is nothing more that can be done for him. With each visit, we add to the ongoing chronicle of his medical status. It's the evidence that we will present after Jesús receives his creative miracle from God that will prove that the Jesús that is gloriously healed is that same boy that once had all of those conditions.

Many times, Jesús asks us for prayer when something overwhelms him. He does it by taking our hand and bringing it to his head, or simply starts by saying loudly, "Father God…" When Andrés and I pray for Jesús, we call him by different names, some of which have been spoken over him prophetically. We declare over him, "You are a healthy, happy boy," "You are an ambassador of Christ," "You are a musician of Heaven," "You are minister of worship," "You are an inspirer of multitudes," and "You are a harvester of miracles." We also say in Hebrew, you are a *bar barakah*, which means a "Son of the blessing."

> It's the evidence that we will present after Jesús receives his creative miracle from God.

When we speak these things in prayer, Jesús smiles and moves back and forth in a joyful dance. He also often quotes Psalm 23 in Spanish, and we are amazed by his memorization of that passage and many others.

Along with this book, we pray it will be a testimony of the Lord's amazing power and grace in our lives—grace and power that is available to you right now. What He has done for us, He will do for you.

Chapter 9

"The best is just to come..."

Andrés

In this book, Marysol and I have shared how we met, fell in love, got married, had children, and came to know Christ as our Messiah, Lord, and Savior. We did this so that you could know us better and know how God worked so sovereignly and lovingly to draw us to a deeper relationship with Christ. But from the very start, our desire was to write a book that introduced you to our Jesucito, to his unusual condition, and to the extraordinary impact he has had on others as our four-leaf clover.

Our son has a purpose. In my understanding of the Bible, I cannot say that God intentionally sent him to Earth with his disabilities, but I *can* say that God will send life and healing through Him as a result of his disabilities. This journey has been a spiritual awakening for me. I now see that God speaks. He has been speaking to us since we learned of Jesús' condition before he was born. I have learned to hear God in the midst of the doctor's prognosis' and opinions, and to trust in His voice of peace and not their words of fear. I believe some medical professionals need to be more sensitive toward life and the things they don't know.

After all, what they do know is less than one-one-hundredth of a percent of what God knows about human beings. I appreciate doctors; they have been helpful and valuable to us. But God always has, and will always have, the last word in every situation.

I remember a couple that we ministered to at a marriage conference FFI conducted in Houston. They were at the point of divorce, their hearts severely hardened toward each other. When they saw Jesús, they were so pleased by him that they forgot themselves as they held him in their arms.

I asked them, "Do you believe God can heal Jesús?"

They both responded without hesitation, "Yes!"

"Then how come," I asked, "you can't believe for your marriage to be restored?"

My question broke their hardness. Today, this couple are leaders in marriage ministry and have a strong relationship. It's often easier to believe in miracles for others, but not for yourself. Don't limit what God can do! If He can perform a creative miracle for Jesús, He certainly can bring healing to your most damaged relationships, to your physical body, or even restoration to your financial situation. The first step is to dare to believe!

> I believe we are the ones commissioned from the Lord to bring Heaven to Earth.

Look again at Isaiah 42:9: "Behold, the former things have come to pass, And new things I declare; Before they spring forth I tell you of them."

All the dreams and the prophetic words that many courageously dared to tell us was God's way of telling us the new things that He is going to do.

Now, pair that truth with this, written by Paul in Romans: "For the earnest expectation of the creation eagerly waits for the revealing of the sons of God. For the creation was subjected to futility, not willingly, but because of Him who subjected it in hope; because the creation itself also will be delivered from the bondage of corruption into the glorious liberty of the children of God. For we know that the whole creation groans and labors with birth pangs together until now. Not only that, but we also who have the first fruits of the Spirit, even we ourselves groan within ourselves, eagerly waiting for the adoption, the redemption of our body." (Romans 8:19-23)

I believe we are the ones commissioned from the Lord to bring Heaven to Earth. We are the ones—and creation is groaning, waiting for us, to wake up and do just that. I recall an amazing analogy comparing God and us to a landlord and its tenant. God is sovereign over the Earth in the same way a landlord is the owner of his apartment complex. When a tenant wants to rent one of his apartments, a contract is made between them and the tenant is given the keys to the apartment. Therefore, the landlord cannot come into the tenant's apartment because it is contractually occupied by the tenant—and the tenant has the *authority* to go in and out of the apartment using the key. In the same way, God has relinquished His authority over the deeds of Earth for a time. but He's going to come back and again be King over His kingdom. Until then, God has given us authority to us like tenants over the Earth to rule over it. The Lord has given the authority to us—and He is awaiting the manifestation of the children of God.

If you are wondering, "What manifestation is that?" I ask you this:

"When was the last time you asked or received a dream from God?" Second Chronicles 7:14 declares, "If My people who are called by My name will humble themselves, and pray and seek

My face, and turn from their wicked ways, then I will hear from heaven, and will forgive their sin and heal their land." That is the manifestation.

God is still doing miracles today—the same big, strong miracles as opening the eyes of the blind, the ears of the deaf, and even raising people from death. We need to dare to believe that the Holy Spirit is working with the same power the apostles had available to them. That has not changed. The power of the Holy Spirit flows through the ages to the generations and all the way to today. I believe revival is coming, and we, the children of God, will manifest it!

People have often come up to us and asked, "But what if Jesús is never healed? Will you still dare to believe?" Marysol and I rejoice in each and every day of Jesús' life, and we know our God is sovereign. We can say, like the blind person in John chapter 9, that Jesús was born for the glory of the Lord to be manifested. If He chooses not to heal Jesús, we will be fine with that.

> God will do what He wants for us—and for Jesús.

God will do what He wants for us—and for Jesús. Whatever He decides, we will serve the One True God!

I've also come to see, and want to tell you, that all of us are four-leaf clovers. Jesús is very unique, but so are our Sofi and Paz. We are all special. No two people are the same. Each one has an amazing, specific purpose from God and is endowed with a deep sense of respect for life. Life belongs to God, and He is the one who brings a deep sense of true hope. This hope does not come from people; it comes from the Lord. He's just waiting for us to come to Him, ask, and then wait on His response according to His will. We have shared many harbingers of the miracle we believe is coming. In the end, Marysol and I believe we—and you—are the harvesters of His miracles because God wants to reveal Himself, and His grace and power, to us and through us each day.

Just dare to believe!

Marysol

I am so thankful to be able to go back through all these years of my life and recognize how faithful and amazing God has been with me and my family—and that He hasn't forsaken us in any way. He has shown us time after time, in so many tangible ways and through so many people, His loving presence. It has been a precious gift to revisit the story of my life and see, through all the joys and all the difficult times, how we have grown in our

> Truth is a person. His name is Jesus.

knowledge of the One who is good, perfect, and so loving. As I walk near to my God, I am more amazed at how much more He wants us to know Him and embrace all He is in us in our daily lives. My purpose in life is to be like Him, walk as He walked on this Earth, not in my own strength but in the power of His Holy Spirit. What a privilege! The Gospel is the only thing that is so simple and at the same time so deep; simple because anyone can understand it but deep because it has the power to transform lives.

At the beginning of this book, Andrés told of searching for an actual four-leaf clover as a boy, but never finding one. Sometimes I have struggled to believe that I could find my four-leaf clover. I thought that maybe I was not one of the chosen ones who could find one for my life. Now, when I recall and see who He is and what He has done, I realize that every one of us—like our Jesucito—is a four-leaf clover. Every day, you can live with expectancy that your life is a unique four-leaf clover to be transformed into His very image as He intended for us in the beginning if we just dare to believe and SEE from His perspective. "And we have known and believed the love that God has for us. God is love, and he who abides in love abides in God, and

God in him." (1 John 4:16, NKJV)

As we are finishing this book I can SEE more clearly than when I was at the beginning of my journey, I was full of fear and thinking with little clarity of God's nature and the message from God that our Jesucito carries. "There is no fear in love; but perfect love casts out fear, because fear involves torment. But he who fears has not been made perfect in love." (1 John 4:18)

I knew it in my mind, but my heart was bound with a lot of chains and doubts, and wrong perceptions about Him, myself. and others. I now can SEE clearer, and I can hardly explain the freedom, joy, and hope I have in my heart for the future. I just know that it is "truth that sets us free." Truth is a person. His name is Jesus.

I am writing about seeing that which I couldn't see before—and it is through Jesús, our little one who is physically blind, that God, in His incredible wisdom, is opening our eyes to really SEE.

I encourage you to take a look at your life journey as I did, and in the middle of it discover the One who loves you, has never forsaken you, and has good and bigger plans for you.

My last word for you is: There is much more than our physical eyes can SEE. Dare to believe!

And this story hasn't ended.

The best is just to come.

"And now abide faith, hope, love, these three; but the greatest of these is love." (1 Corinthians 13:13, NKJV)

We want to thank the following people who sponsored the publication of
A Four-Leaf Clover: A Harbinger of Miracles

Dear Sponsors,

Thank you for your generous donation to our book. Without your support we would not have been able to complete this project. To you, we want to dedicate the words that the Lord Jesus Christ said in Acts 20:35: "It is more blessed to give than to receive."

Adriana Correa	México	Diego Robalino	Ecuador
Alex Shiva	USA	Don & Patty Geisler	USA
Alvaro Vázquez	Ecuador	Edie Hurley	USA
Ana Patricia Pesqueira	México	Elda Nora Esponda	México
Angie Fernandez	USA	Enrique Rivera	USA
Beatriz de la C	México	Erica Bernal	México
Bernhard Laubli	USA	Estefania Cevallos	USA
Bernice Roll	USA	Fabricio Malo	Ecuador
Betita Cordero Vázquez	Ecuador	Familia Bonilla Cevallos	Ecuador
Bill & Connie McDonald	Ecuador	Fausto Moncayo	Ecuador
Bob and Jan Cass	USA	Hannah Stevens	USA
Cathy Tesi	USA	Hernan Barahona	Ecuador
Claudio Patiño	Ecuador	Jaime Rios	Ecuador
Craig & Jan Hill	USA	Jeff & Judy Allen	USA
Crawford Family	USA	Jen Anderson	USA
Debi Resner	USA	Jessica Gutai	USA
Dennis & Kathy Watson	USA	Jessica y Gerónimo	USA
Diego José Vazquez	Ecuador	Jim & Jan McSheffrey	USA

Jim & Linda Floyd	USA	Pablo Vázquez Rosales	Ecuador
John & Claudia Gross	USA	Paola Rovalino	Ecuador
John and Patsy Martinez	USA	Patricia Loyola	México
Jonathon A. Humig	USA	Pedro Crespo	Ecuador
Jorge Loyola	México	Pedro Malo Vázquez	Ecuador
José Antonio Alsina	México	Pedro Miranda	Ecuador
Juan Carlos y Martha Durazo	USA	Pete Fox	USA
Juan Fernando Cordero	Ecuador	Rafael Canez	USA
Judy Otis Fry	USA	Randy & Danielle Baethge	USA
Kalvin Baker	USA	Raul Troya	Ecuador
Larry & Nancy Howery	USA	Ron & Luisa Ogan	USA
Luis Anaya	México	Ron & Sharon Quarles	USA
Ma Paulina Cisneros	Ecuador	Rosey Koberlein	USA
Maria E. Araujo	Ecuador	Sam Trexler	USA
Mary Ortiz Vidal	Ecuador	Sergio Ramos	Ecuador
Mauricio "Don Malo"	Ecuador	Shelby Rambaud	USA
Mauricio Vázquez Cueva	Ecuador	Susan Mendez	USA
Moira Wristen	USA	Susana Ordoñez Vintimilla	Ecuador
Nancy Velasco	USA	Tío Juan	Ecuador
Neftalí & Myrna Cabrera	USA	Tomás Loose	México
Nora Elizabeth Vázquez	Ecuador	Toño Vázquez	Ecuador
Osmar Jimenez	USA	Vonda Rhodes	USA

About the Authors

Andrés and Marysol Malo have been married for 20 years, Andrés is from Ecuador and Marysol is from Mexico, and they have three wonderful children, Paz (18), Jesús (16) and Sofi (15). Andrés and Marysol were the founders of FAICE, a non-profit organization to help blind children in Ecuador. Looking for a specialized education for their son Jesús, they migrated to the United States in 2007, invited by Family Foundations International, as missionaries and as National Hispanic Coordinators to train teams and establish a culture of blessing in families. They have conducted seminars dedicated to strengthening family relationships and to restoring the value of covenant in marriage. Many of those have been translated in Spanish. They are also being used by God to be a liaison between the Anglo and the Hispanic culture in the nation. Andrés is a real estate agent in Arizona, and Marysol is in the process of becoming a professional life coach through the Professional Christian Coach Institute. Both participate actively in their local church, Passion Church, and with organizations dedicated to improve the quality of life of people living in Tucson, AZ.